This autobiography is written with lifelong gratitude to Professor Nick Brooks, Professor Ed Ingamells, Professor Dan Strauss — and everyone who trains and fights for Mill Hill BJJ, the greatest Brazilian Jiu-Jitsu academy in the world.

Reader's note: This book is in no way a training instruction manual. All of my personal insights about fighting technique should be taken with a pinch of salt. If I'm an expert in anything, it's in getting beaten up by my opponents over and over and over again, while trying to retain a smile on my face. But therein lies growth.

PROLOGUE

I'm 12 years old and sat in my best friend's bedroom, overwhelmed by nausea. It's 4am. Cigarette smoke fills the room. I'm not really used to being up at this time — when I used to live next door before we moved home a year ago, I was usually in bed and asleep by 9pm, tucked under my Knight Rider duvet cover.

Nevertheless here I am, squinting at a small old TV screen while my best friend and former neighbour plays Sonic the Hedgehog on his games console.

All I really want to do is go to sleep (and go home).

But I'm 12. I don't know myself yet. And I want to keep up appearances. I want to look hard. At least I think I do, even if, against all odds, I've already started my furious early descent into male pattern balding.

My best friend has also changed recently. He's become 'street' to fit in with the other kids at his school, one of whom is also sat next to me on this sofa. This other friend is not so much into video games as preying on and beating up children weaker than him. Kids like me.

The joke's on him ultimately however because I looked him up on Facebook recently and he looks like Mr. Blobby.

Behind the sofa I'm lying across, there's an older, skinnier, athletic boy who's on the cusp of becoming a man.

He's 17, and he's outstanding at kickboxing, obsessed with it. Often he'll ask us younger boys to run at him while he takes us out with semi-hard Bruce Lee-style kicks to the body and head.

We do this because we're 12, and we've seen countless, unbelievably poorly dubbed Jackie Chan movies on VHS, so we take the older boy's lead.

Either way, it hurts when he kicks us, but I'm young, I've got some spirit in me. Often I find myself charging towards him like a huge blur of double chin and passion. I just don't like the getting hit part.

Yet as I sit here at one end of my friend's sofa, dropping in and out of exhausted attentiveness, the smell of Benson & Hedges cigarettes knocking me sick, I'm struck by the thought that my parents would be horrified if they saw me still up at this time in the morning.

A missile of sorts hits the back of my head.

I ignore it at first, and hope it might be a mistake. But nope, now something else hits me on the bonce. This time it's not a half-empty 10-packet of fags, but a box of matches.

I sit up and look around. My former best friend, and the bully who preys on weaker children and the 17-year-old Bruce Lee wannabe all laugh. That missile was genuinely meant for my head.

"Could you please stop?" I recall saying (though it was probably something far less assertive and mature).

Another missile is hurled at my head. And then another. The laughter surrounding me builds to a crescendo.

I feel my face turn beetroot red. I'm so embarrassed. They know I'm weaker than them, mentally and physically. They have the edge of intimidation on their side, the willingness, I presume at that age, to go further in a fight or any altercation than I would even consider. I'm soft. Conflict is new to me. I don't know the rules, the terms of life's deal, or have the experience to handle these deep waters. I'm drowning.

I'm also incapacitated by fear, with my arms and legs feeling like heavy poles. I realise I'm shouting a bit, and getting teary now. But my insistence for them to stop laughing at me is not getting through.

And so I shout a bit louder, my little posh voice only exacerbating my weak otherness in their eyes. I'm now running at the older boy who'd started throwing all this ordnance at my head, the kickboxing 17-year-old. 'What the hell am I doing?' I'm thinking. 'Not important: keep running!'

In my mind I can also hear the words of my boxing fan Dad,

saying: "If you're ever in a fight, keep moving forward! Don't ever, ever, ever take a step backwards."

Which sounds like great advice, if you're cornering Mike Tyson or someone actually schooled in the art of hitting and not getting hit.

The problem is that the advice echoing in my mind actually came from someone who I'd later realise has never been in a single physical confrontation he's won, just like me up to this point.

Because boy, if my dad had won a fight, you could bet he would have worked that into our family's mythology! And he hasn't.

Instead I was fed stories about how my dad's dad had avoided fighting abroad in World War Two by pretending to be able to play the tuba, and joining the army band. Even though he couldn't play a single note, there he was in the British Military's marching band, allegedly, honking away out of key, prancing down the promenade near their home in Brighton, disgruntling all the serious musicians around him.

Granted, it's a funny notion, but it was an act underscored by cowardice. My grandfather cowered out of fighting. Add that to the fact that my father never had any idea how to defend himself other than gritting his teeth and growling when I'd been naughty as a child, and what you have there is a family lineage of complete non-fighters. A family of anti-Rocky's.

But right in this moment, intoxicated by fantasies of 'holding the centre of the ring' like a 1950s prize-fighter defending his title at Madison Square Garden, I went for broke.

Fuck it, 'Little Me' reasoned — my dad's nearly 50 at this point, and I'm 12. Dad must be right. He knows the man code!? He's a grown man, isn't he? You don't get to be that bold and confident unless you've passed all of puberty's gatekeepers, surely. So, I doubled down on my faith in my dad's brain farts.

Hence my decision to run at the kickboxing 17-year-old who threw all those things at my head. Look at me go: I am a bloody mini He-Man.

But two things happen: 1) I don't throw a single punch at him as the idea of balling up my fist and punching someone to hurt them physically in any way feels morally wrong and I've never done that before in my life; and 2) I feel a blisteringly hot pain around the tip of my willy, like my helmet is about to be ripped off by the lock jaws of a German Shepherd.

Very quickly, I realise that I'm being simultaneously pinned against a wardrobe and lifted off my feet. It appears that the kickboxing 17-year-old is hoisting me up by both the tip of my willy's bell-end and my right nipple.

It's not just a humiliating way to be subdued: it's beginning to feel like I'm having the tip of my penis slowly guided towards the centre of a Bunsen burner's flame.

Either way, I'm incapable of fighting back. I want my penis back. As a 12-year-old I haven't even used it yet, and already it's being removed from my person. And my left tit is now in complete agony, being twisted and twisted, redefining the parameters of what it means to be at the receiving end of the world's most ruthless nipple cripple. It feels like a Chinese Burn, but across my breast, like my tit fat's being wrung out of its skin as if through a cake icing bag.

Amidst the pain, the truth hits me hard: why did I even bother running at this kid anyway? What was I hoping to achieve? Never mind my penis and nipple. This kid could have Jackie Channed me to death.

Moments later, I find myself sat back on the sofa, seemingly having been hoisted back to my previous sitting place by my genitals. I'm a broken little boy.

The fracas has subdued, and the other boys have laughed themselves disinterested.

As the sun begins to rise on a new morning, I bed down on that sofa I'd been lying on when the missiles had started landing.

I quietly sob myself to sleep, my tears burning humiliation into my young, puffy face.

In that moment I felt extremely alone. Where had my best friend been to support me, to tell these bigger boys to stop their bullying and laughing at me? Why hadn't my best friend, who'd brought these tougher boys into my world, told them to stop? I was a good boy. An innocent boy. An over-thinker, a worrier, and definitely not a fighter. I'd never expressed myself through violence my whole life. And for being a good, mild-mannered child, I'd gotten humiliated and abused.

When you're that age, you don't have the birds-eye view of life to say: these kids are also the victims; they're probably just very unhappy themselves at home.

Instead, as a child, you look at these kids in pure terror; in that nervous way where your stomach is telling you that anything can happen in the world because as a 12-year-old you've only begrudgingly came to terms with the fact that magic isn't real half a decade earlier. You're still a baby in the big scheme of things.

You don't know how the world works. The rawness and viciousness of children can lead to anywhere in your childish mind. And so, unless you're courageous, you get trampled on by the what-ifs that run riot in your head.

But, looking back, what got me most about this whole situation was that I'd felt betrayed. No, really: why hadn't my best friend jumped in? He was my one link to the normality of the outside world — my one lifeline to order — and he'd watched in silence as I'd been manhandled.

He was a good kid, really; a nice boy. For all his posturing and mine at that age, we couldn't have hurt a fly.

But someone, somehow, I remember thinking, should have intervened at the point where I was getting smacked around for sport and said: "Stop. What you're doing now will rearrange this young boy's personality forever."

But no one did intervene. Because there is no Superman who's going to come and save us. We all have to fight our battles alone.

The problem, I soon came to realise, was that I hadn't known how to defend myself. And the boys taunting me had known it — those shits could smell my weakness.

And as would eventually become apparent to me in later life, the moment bullies realise you won't fight back, that's when they prey even harder on you.

Deep down, therefore, I knew I needed to get tougher; to grow up to become the kind of sailor who could shave his balls in a storm without drawing blood.

It would nevertheless take another quarter of a century for that realisation to completely click in my mind.

And good Lord did I suffer along the way

CHAPTER ONE

Even in adulthood I've always dreamt of being able to take care of myself, probably because I have terrible asthma and I've read too many Andy McNab books.

Most of my life I've been overweight and so I also had such low self-esteem that I'd wrap it up in a personality that just told lots of jokes to obscure the issue. I was also traumatised by the fact that the nanny who helped raise me said I had a bubble butt when I was six, and took it upon herself to draw on a piece of paper just how my bottom juts out from my back like a vertical Bell curve, and then swoops back round to my legs.

After only six years in the world, I'd been told by one of the only people I trusted that I had an arse like a horse. And the problem is, there's an element of truth in that, even now. Hence the fact I never tuck my shirt in, and my wife (and nowadays even my young children) occasionally calling me, 'Bubble butt.'

In fact, my wife says I've got an arse like that bloke who wears cut off denim shorts and high heels in that moneysupermarket.com advert on TV.

But the joke's on them, really, because my wife agreed to marry me, and my children haven't learnt about genetics in school yet.

So, what with my big arse, and my congenital cowardice, the idea of being terrified of fighting has run through me for most of my life.

Though, from a physical aspect, God knows why. A punch in the face, after all, just feels a bit sharp then numb — it's the shock of that first crack in the chops that hurts so much, though really it's just your manliness shaking in its boots.

Meanwhile, a full-on scrap I'd soon learn just feels sweaty, and basically, if you give the fight some breathing space, it's actually quite thrilling.

Still, all I wanted to do as I got older was to feel adequately prepared that if I was started on by someone, I could defend myself, preferably by either doing the Jean-Claude Van Damme splits or his flappy leg kick thing in my opponent's face. Alternatively, I quite liked the idea of having a fight like Steven Seagal in a biker bar, flapping and slapping and spinning people around pool tables, while also somehow managing to eat 9,000 calories before brunch.

The problem is, we are thankfully duty-bound by society not to fight and hit people because it's anti-social, quite rightly, and violent. And so unless it's under the right circumstances, you will go to jail.

So rather than finding out if I could defend myself, instead I fantasised about being Neo in The Matrix, and knowing Kung-Fu. Just without the 15 years it probably takes to become any good at it.

Unfortunately though, I was still imprisoned in this self-image I had of myself of being absolutely useless in the face of real violence, probably because I knew I wasn't prepared to go where tougher men might (like lifting someone up by the tip of his penis, say).

Back in that smoke-filled bedroom, I'd sworn by my father's mantra of, "keep swinging and going forward", and rather than getting the shit beaten out of me, I'd practically been circumcised for a second time. My dad's solution hadn't worked for me. And in fact, after I'd applied it 'in theatre' it just had no real-world application, his theory collapsing in on itself like a chocolate teapot.

So I swung the other way. I knew I had a duty to myself to learn how to fend off the bullies. But I also had a strong desire to not get my entire face ripped off by a bully and worn as a mask.

Consequently, feigning toughness became my next port of call. I began lifting weights; heavy weights that saw me slip two vertebrae and take a year out of exercise because when I walked it felt like my entire upper body might slide off my hips and onto the floor. My hope when I was 'back at the weights', therefore, was that people would see my alleged 'gains' (just more fat, really) and not bother starting on me.

But that didn't work either. People would still occasionally bump into me uncaringly during commutes. They'd occasionally start on me in the street, for a variety of reasons. I'd still have people in discos shine lights on my bald head to laugh at the reflection (before, hopefully, getting their retinas seared off their eyeballs by the brilliant reflection of light from my massive bald bonce).

Bullies could see my weakness in my eyes. For all my posturing and blubber masquerading as muscle, I was still shit scared. Fear has a stench that clings to you like the smell of wet chips on a fat bloke.

My so-called childhood friends had stamped over the only fighting code I knew of. Now, instead of coming forward at them relentlessly, as my dad had suggested, my code was: if you go forward throwing punches, you're going to get hurt.

That said, I did join a local boxing gym and tried to hide the fact I like reading by acting like a cockney and saying things like, "Wibbley wobbly wibbley, ten for a pound! Naughty!"
But basically, I just got shouted at for being a – and I quote – "fat bucket of shit" who couldn't do more than three sit-ups, and I sweated so much that afterwards my face looked like I'd emerged from a salt mine.

To make matters worse, I was still haunted by something I saw as a young boy that further compounded the notion in my young mind that if you wanted to know how to defend yourself, you should probably listen to someone who can actually fight.

Never was this truer than when, aged six — and again involving my father — I saw the local dry cleaner, this man-mountain of hairy arms and bleach-scented denim, affectionately put my dad in a half-nelson until my father, my original role model, was begging to be let go.

I can't tell you how badly that screwed up my impressionable mind when I saw that. "Oh, look, there's my dad, my Superman, begging for mercy from a very stranger who's taller than Jaws from the Roger Moore Bond films, but dressed like Status Quo, with a full head of hair on each forearm."

After all, what kind of relationship was built on an idea that at some point, you'd repeatedly end up getting your arm practically broken behind your back? And yet this was the basis of their so-called friendship, because he did this to my dad all the time. And I hate to sound like an after-timer, but I didn't exactly see my dad going forward and throwing non-stop punches and "keep coming forward." Unless of course you interpret 'coming forward throwing punches' as having one arm locked behind your back while you shout, beggingly, "Ooh, ooh, ooh, ah, ah, ah" like a slightly demented version of Sting.

No. For a child to witness that happening to his dad was torture. But it just reinforced in my mind that, hey, perhaps I'm not from a family of people who can defend themselves. What did I know? I was nine (though already balding).

Add to that the fact that I spent my teenage years being repeatedly mugged or marched to the newsagents by a bully on the threat of violence in order to buy them cigarettes, and overall my impression of fighting was that I was a victim. The kind of victim that when he was 13 would be often approached by groups of older kids and told to jump up and down so that they could hear whether the money I may have hidden in my shoes would jingle.

I was a wide-open goal for muggers. Often when they'd ask for my watch I'd have to come up with some cockamamie story about how my dying great-great-grandmother had given it to me on her deathbed, and I'd at least see some humanity enter into the eyes of my mugger (before ultimately shrugging and just stealing my Velcro-fastened Rip Curl wallet instead).

So often I'd walk around not just susceptible to getting picked on and beaten up, but also to the prospect of leaving the house with a few quid's pocket money and knowing it's likely I'd come home broke.

Being a fat chubber didn't help either. When I wasn't in my hometown of London getting mugged, I was on holiday with my parents swimming with my t-shirt on and telling everyone I just had really badly burnt shoulders so I was covering up. Just so no sunbathing Dads saw me topless and muttered, 'Jugs!' as I swam past. So really, what with my having a pair of chubby boobs as a teenager and getting perpetually mugged in the street, you could say I had it all going for me.

So there you have it. A childhood spent giving away my money and self-esteem instead of fighting to defend them. And as I grew older, things only got worse.

CHAPTER TWO

Knowing that you're such a massive wimp affects you over time, let me tell you. You become soft, scared, and weak. You really do. You quietly pray that you'll never be dragged into an altercation. Because what would you do if you were?

And as you get older, that mind-set subsumes you. When bigger men look at you, you struggle to hold their gaze. Big or small, no one can be bothered to start on someone who looks up for it, size be damned. But that wasn't me.

So, my default mode of self-defence became just staring into the face of any assailant with a flappy expression like I was going through a wind tunnel but no sound was coming out of my mouth. I'd just stand there getting accosted in the street and shit my pants.

Of course, if I ever saw something untoward going on in the street — for example, a man arguing unfairly with his girlfriend — I'd always feel the need to jump in and say something. I've always known what was right and wrong. But that didn't mean I wouldn't completely shake in my boots when I did.

There were two sides to my personality: the side that wanted to be the hero, and the side that wanted to run to the hills, screaming in fear.

I was 50% my father's son still, while the other half wanted to find a new way of seeing the world, of being able to defend myself on my own terms.

By my mid-twenties, in fact, many of my friends had evolved into Mini-Me versions of their parents, and all the accompanying neuroses that entailed. But me, I wanted to become my own man. Especially after, in my early twenties, I'd been beaten up in front of my girlfriend outside a nightclub by a man with one arm. Once that happened, as he leaned over my collapsed state, pulverising me with his one fist, that's when I realised that I was no man at all.

How could I protect my girlfriend who soon became my fiancé and ultimately my wife who laughed at my large buttocks — as well as the mother of my children — when I couldn't even defend us from a man with one arm? How would I ever be able to protect our future children when I was still a child myself? I didn't want to end up becoming the husband who gets beaten up by a burglar in the entrance to his home in the middle of the night while still naked and with an accidental semi after hearing a few whispers downstairs. I wanted to be The Man. Not The Man Who Cowers Behind His Wife. Or worse still, The Man Whose Wife Is His Shield. I wanted to have the strength of character and confidence to be able to fight our battles for the both of us.

And then, one night in my 39th year, as I was walking home from the train station after work, it happened. I had a ridiculously large gym bag with me. I'd been lifting weights. But I was older now, and my close beard was greying.

Ahead of me, coming down the hill towards me, there was this other guy, dishevelled and a bit older than me, running for the train station. He was late for something. And he looked angry about it. As he ran past me, he banged into my bag, as if to say, "Get the hell out of my way..."

In my mind, he saw an easy access point straight through me to the station and so he effectively just tried to run into me. And so he blew past me and knocked my own bag into me. Offended, I instinctively shouted, "Oy!"

He stopped in his tracks, turned around then paced towards me. He squared up to me, looking me deep in my eyes. His eyes were smiling slightly as if we both knew he was prepared to go further in a fight than I was (even though he probably also had absolutely no idea how to fight; not properly anyway).

And so, I froze. I knew how to throw a few standard boxing combinations because I'd done a fair few boxercise classes by now. But hitting the pads of a boxing instructor that also don't hit you back as Bruce Lee might say, and artfully hitting a live opponent who's genuinely trying to hurt you, are two very separate things.

So although I knew I could allegedly throw a punch, when it came to crunch time I could feel all the confidence drain out of my legs.

Deep down, I knew that if it came to an actual scuffle, there was no guarantee that I wouldn't get absolutely pulverised.

The train station is on a hill near my home and so you walk up to the exit through a narrow, long, poorly lit alleyway that's highly built up on either side, as if you're travelling down a long river before being spat out onto the busy pavement and road ahead.

All the other commuters seemed to dissipate.

It was me, this bloke with the glint in his eye who was a bit taller and fatter than me leering over me, and that was basically it. There'd be no one else there that I could call out to and squeal for help. I'd be done for.

"...Right, I'm calling the police," I mumbled, as if indignant that society could have stooped so low. But really I was absolutely fretting.

The spark receded in his eyes, leading to an expression that looked something like bemusement, and then he slowly drew away from me, turned his back on me as he continued walking to the station, then turned back to look at me stood further on up the hill and screamed, "Prick!"

And to be fair, he had a point. I'd also just spent the last year learning on and off how to do Panantukan, the close quarter-combat fighting techniques that Jason Bourne uses in his films to dispatch rival relentless assassins.

Well, let's just say, Panantukan in the real world doesn't evolve like that. At. All. What was I going to do? Fight this guy with a small betting shop biro and a rolled-up copy of 'Diabetic Living' magazine? No. Of course not. Instead I completely lost my nerve.

When I got home, I immediately looked up on the Internet whether it would have been legal for me to throw the first punch, not that I would have done as it would have seemed far too much of an over-commitment to go down the route of violence, which scared me.

But I was furious. And although the law on this was pretty vague — all violence in response to a threat, it seems, has to be proportionate, and proportionate is a relative term — really, deep down, I knew the truth. When push had nearly come to shove, I'd just stood there trembling.

I was now a grown man, nearly 40. Had I not learnt anything about how to defend myself and my spirit in the 28 years since I was beaten up at my best friend's house while his mate nearly ripped my bell-end off? Nope, it seemed not.

This was almost the final straw for me — the moment when I realised, no, actually, it's a rough world out there, I need to genuinely learn how to fight, or at least be able to defend myself in a credible way where I can control a marauding madman sufficiently enough for him not to kill me.

But I failed to act upon this insight, and my ego paid for it yet again a few months later.

I was out with my wife and two daughters on a sunny Sunday afternoon. I was parked up just alongside a park so that my two under five-year-olds could climb over the face of a giant wooden worm. And then I heard the shuffling, scraping of feet behind me.

As I had my head, shoulders and arms in the backseat fiddling with the seatbelt of one of my kids as she tried to stick her fingers between one of my eyelids and eyeball, I could feel my Spidey Sense start tingling. I just felt like I was about to come under threat.

So as I was fiddling with a child-seat belt buckle, I turned my head round to see who was coming up behind and alongside me. My wife had just gotten out of the car on the driver's side and was walking around the front of the car with my other daughter.

And then I saw him.

He wasn't a big bloke: not at all. But he was angry, rough-looking, like he'd already experienced a long history of being unloved. He had bloodshot eyes, and dishevelled greasy hair.

Despite it being a warm summer's afternoon, he was dressed for a hip-hop winter. He was carrying a blue plastic off-license bag with cans of what looked like lager in. He brought with him the stench of weed.

I looked at him then slowly withdrew myself from out of the backseats of my car, to protect myself I suppose in case he decided to jump me or my family while I was half-in and half-out of the car.

My stomach was doing backflips and I had the taste of battery acid rising in my throat.

"What the fuck are you looking at?" he shouted, eyeballing me from a metre away, as he walked past. "Go back to your kids. Or I'll scratch your eyes out with a key."

Well. It's hard to really describe how this incident made me feel. I was scared, certainly. But was I to blame? Had I flashed him some primal defensive facial expression that suddenly made him feel so threatened he wanted to make me look like a pirate? I don't think so. I just think he was furious with the state of his life.

But that's not the point. I had little doubt that he would have certainly tried to carry out his threat if push had come to shove. And he acknowledged that I had kids with me, so any physical altercation was in essence totally inappropriate. And yet he'd threatened to blind their father in front of them without any genuine consideration for the psychological well-being of my children.

From nowhere he'd brought violence into their world, the equivalent of leaving a decapitated unicorn's head in their bedsheets. He'd briefly pulled back the curtain on the innocence of my children to reveal a world of war, injustice, violence, famine, poor mental health and totally inappropriate gherkins in McDonald's cheeseburgers. Screw this guy.

He kept walking. He didn't look back. But I was shaken. Make no mistake about that. And so were my wife and daughters. That bloke had ruined our day. He'd pulled the sun down out of the clouds, wiped his arse on it and shoved it back into the sky.

And although he was probably going to go back to his fag-filled world of Grand Theft Auto, microwaved spaghetti carbonaras and big, sobbing wanks, that didn't make me feel any better. Not at all. If this crusty little bastard had gone for me, I'd have been completely powerless.

Now almost half way through my life, I really, finally, needed to do something about this. "Keep swinging and going forward" was an ideology that had failed me. And so too had staring at my assailant with the look of someone who's gone into rigour mortis while struggling with constipation. No, this was getting ridiculous, I reasoned. The world, for all its summer barbecues and smoky-voiced food adverts, was a rough place, with tension and the threat of violence only ever one layer below the surface of our everyday lives. In fact, if it wasn't for the rule of law, I came to understand, we'd all be running round like zombies, hunting each other and cooking our neighbours. No. I needed to do something about this.

And so, like the long line of history's victims, I didn't. And things got worse.

CHAPTER THREE

A well as being traumatised by my own lifelong cowardice in the face of danger, by this time in my adult life I was also going through a particularly rough time professionally.

I'd grown tired of the company that I'd been working for repeatedly relaunching itself with my involvement to ever-declining sales. It was in the magazine industry; a sector that like newspapers was being obliterated by the Internet and all its free content.

Who wants to pay £5 for a magazine when there's much shorter, more succinct content, often that you don't have to laboriously read but can watch, for free - on your phone! Which was fair enough.

But when all you know is how to make horseshoes, and people start driving cars instead of riding horses, it not only takes the industry years to come to terms with this truth - you're left with an entire industry of people who'd prefer to stick their heads in the sand, rather than come to terms with that giant iceberg up ahead.

I was now one of those ostriches. However, coming to terms with the fact that your skills are now fundamentally useless, for all the sweat, and heartbreak and turmoil that comes with any professional career, is heart-breaking.

But I was as slow to adapt to this fact as I was to finally adjust to the realisation that I'd now spent more than a quarter of a century being scared of getting beaten up. I felt like a failure both professionally and as a man.

And so, as the magazine I worked at began to plummet ever new depths sales-wise, ever-newer bosses were brought in to 'save the magazine!' And eventually my face didn't fit in anymore.

Of course, like all stoic heroes, I took this in fairly good stride by having an absolute fricking meltdown in private. I'd often find myself staring into the distance, thinking, half-angrily, "Well, they'll see it's a losing battle...They'll see..." Like all cowards, I wanted revenge.

And they did see. The people who had made me feel like an unchanged man in changing times were themselves squeezed out two years later. But when that happened, I didn't do the vindication victory lap that I thought I would when my professional executors got moved on. Not at all. In fact, that moment of revenge went by in a blip of consciousness.

Instead, life just went on as normal. The birds were still in the trees getting poisoned by all the passing cars. The sun was out. I still woke up feeling a lumbering heaviness about the world. I still had chunky, Pepperami-shaped nipples.

My personality was still the same: I still carried the same rock of injustice on my back and I couldn't cut it off. What was happening to me?

The magazine had now collapsed and gone out of print, completely eradicating 12 years of my professional life, and I didn't feel any vindication. I didn't even feel any pity or sadness. All my friends at that magazine had also been squeezed out, thankfully, I suppose, before having to see their life's work go down the toilet on the magazine's final day. And all I felt was numb.

And then it hit me: maybe my heaviness about my life wasn't solely about my tumultuous magazine career as well as my inability to stand to for myself my entire life.

Maybe it was...oh my god, how lame.

That's it! I was having a mid-life crisis.

Now the term 'mid-life crisis' gets bandied about a lot in Western culture as if it's no biggie; as if it's completely innocuous and benign to start considering getting a hair transplant and buying cowboy boots.

Except it really is a big deal. And when a mid-life crisis has got you in its clutches, you end up physically and emotionally destroyed by it, just like Leonardo DiCaprio was in The Revenant when he was nearly dry-humped to death by that bear.

I'd look at younger people and think, "Why are you so happy?"

To my mind, they didn't know the secret; that it's all a hoax. That after the exams and grades of school then university and the promise of a bright tomorrow comprised of who-the-heck-knows-at-20?, life would slip perfectly into place. The universe would mould around my personality. I wouldn't have to necessarily strive for things, and get repeatedly shat in the face for my efforts, or physically threatened, as seems to be the standard hallmark of a life well lived. No, in my mind, all you had to do was 'believe to achieve.'

Which sounds like nonsense just writing it. My illusion of life first started crumbling the moment I asked my dad at the age of six whether Father Christmas was real. And he replied, "Well, put it like this: he's sleeping with your mother..." And then the descent just gets steeper and steeper, until the best you can really hope for in life is to not get blown up on a train on your daily commute, and a quiet moment of reflection in the disabled toilets at work. Before ushering another pointless day goodbye by eating a 4pm pack of steak-flavoured McCoy's.

And yet, that's not how you see life when you're coming up through it, when you're breakdance fighting some other gonad in a hipster bar somewhere or dressing like a funky bin man or sailor because that's fashion, yeah?

Life, as they say, seems to be something that happens to you, rather than you taking it by the reigns and bending it to your will. Of course you have to pretend that you're in control of it, that you can horse-whisper its limitations down to a pace and reality that you're happy with. You do have to actually try your hardest, for your own self-respect if anything. But if you come out of university and think the world is going to throw you a congratulations party similar to Barack Obama's election victory party just because you've finished your studies, you've got another thing coming.

And that's the great shock about life: it's not a computer game. You don't go through all the various ever-higher levels of education with all their stresses, finally get to the Big Boss — your degree dissertation — smash his head in, and then clock life. Absolutely not. You beat the Big Boss, but the computer game isn't over. You get sent straight back to the beginning of the game with a completely new set of rules and a whole bunch of different end-of-level bosses; and unlike the former game — Education — where it potentially undermined your confidence in certain boring subjects that you were just a bit less competent in, this new game is just one massive wincefest as you grit your teeth and just try to get through it…

Or so I thought. You see, it was while noodling my way through potential podcasts to listen to in order to transcend such existential desperation that I stumbled upon Jocko Podcast, hosted by former Navy SEAL Jocko Willink. That's when the fog began to lift.

This Jocko guy didn't just look like he could fight — he's a bona fide axe-murderer who's seen more strife through the lens of war than I could ever imagine. And amazingly he'd come out of it the other side laughing.

Which in itself is a bit worrying. For a man who says he's killed over 500 'bad guys' — itself a worrying statement because it presumes that only one side in war has the monopoly on morality — he seems remarkably content. Only a person who's been brainwashed into believing he's the good guy can murder with such impunity, not feeling a moment's regret for the murders he's caused. Me, I'd be lying in bed each night trying to imagine the morality of taking someone's life — and whether or not they had children. Or if, in fact, I was actually the bad guy. Then trying to eliminate that thought from my mind.

Yet despite such concerns, I too soon became indoctrinated with his 'I'm only here to win' philosophy. Soon, I began to fanatically obsess over Jocko Willink's philosophy on life.

Because the lessons about life he did learn from war were life-changing, certainly for me; mainly, his idea that if the world is becoming too overwhelming, and all your obligations are piling up on you, and the people around you are going crazy, and panicking, and blaming you…WHATEVER.

Just keep your shape and carry on with your disciplines. DIS-

CIPLINE EQUALS FREEDOM is his slogan. And in many ways, I couldn't agree more. Although I did go through a patch of having so many disciplines to do each day that I nearly had a mental breakdown — "Oh, God. It's 10pm on a Tuesday and I still haven't meditated yet! And I've still got to mow the lawn!!" So maybe don't go totally crazy with it.

That said, what I really took from Jocko's podcast, and what I was really hunting for when I stumbled upon it, wasn't necessarily a code of conduct and a way through which I could lead my life.

No, what I really wanted to know was, what does someone like Jocko, a silver star-winning master in the art of war, think the best way of defending yourself in a fight is, say, for example, when you're 13 and getting picked on by your best friend's friends?

Or when you're about to get beaten up, at the age of 39, by a big hairy bloke in an alleyway outside a tube station, and your stomach feels tighter than a mouse's rectum.

Then what? What would Jocko advise was the best form of self-defence?

Listening to his podcast, Jocko was unequivocal: it's Brazilian Jiu-Jitsu.

Why? Because unlike most martial arts, BJJ starts on the ground, where nearly every fight ends up. Which means the moment you end up on the floor, that's where you come into your own, either by choking the life out of someone with your arms or their clothes, or cranking someone's joints in such an awesomely unpleasant nature that they're begging for mercy.

It is the antithesis of Kung-Fu or any other traditional martial art where you're spinning through the air. It anticipates the fact that you're going to be taken down to the ground. And then, that's where your game starts, whether you're grinding your weight over someone until they accidentally offer you a limb to grab as your opponents thrust their arms out to defend themselves from your oncoming mass.

Of course, there is a version of Jiu-Jitsu practiced by the Japanese and used by their police force to incapacitate criminals under arrest.

It involves wrist locks and other horrendously painful ways of twisting an opponent's entire fist back up his own buttocks. And I suppose, in essence, it's practical in some situations where the other person is putting up minimal resistance.

But what happens when someone's coming at you full throttle with foaming spit obscuring their chin as they throw haymakers at your face? What then? Say to them: "Would you mind standing still for a second while I just remember the eight different parts of this interrelated technique that only works on an inert person?"

No. Of course you don't. That approach doesn't work. And what happens if both you and your attacker end up collapsed on top of each other, wriggling and thrashing around as you both attempt to simultaneously attack and defend yourself? That's not a scenario where you can suddenly pull out some karate kata moves you learnt when you were nine years old, is it?

Because really, how are you going to get the leverage to throw a punch anyway, no matter how lame and half-cocked, if you haven't got your legs underneath you to throw it?

And dare I say it: what would Bruce Lee have done if someone had actually rugby-tackled him off his feet? Yes, he could do awesome spinny kicks and flappy-flappy stuff with his legs. And there's no doubt that his close-quarter hand-blocking-fist-throwing stuff looked awesome in the movies.

But what does a man who only kicks and punches do when he's been knocked over and is flat on his back?

That's what I now realise about all these martial arts. Yes, they're fine in theory and they look spectacular in films. They even feel cool when someone's teaching them to you.

But as I later learnt had already been demonstrated in the first few Ultimate Fighting Championship (UFC) cage-fights, the moment the fight is taken to the ground, as they almost always inevitably are as competing fighters knock each other off balance, there's only one martial art that actually ends up prevailing across all disciplines.

And the name of that combat sport? Brazilian Jiu-Jitsu.

CHAPTER FOUR

And so, there I had it: the mission had been lain before me. If I wanted to undo four decades of hard-core pant-soiling in the face of confrontation, learning BJJ was the terrifying adventure into the unknown that I had to embark on.

In many ways, it was a mission to rescue my innocent child-like self from the clutches of all those bullies who'd sniffed out my weakness and pounced. And actually, the prospect of being able to learn a form of self-defence where I could vicariously imagine defending myself with awesome skill in all of those previous scenarios from my past that had traumatised me felt thrilling. Imagine becoming a master at fighting then being able to go back in time to confront your past enemies with your new skills, thereby saving your future self, a bit like in The Terminator?

And yet, when I looked up Jiu-Jitsu on YouTube, it looked terrifying.

Firstly those guys doing it looked so physically athletic, jumping and moving and rolling around all over each other. And my body felt so physically rigid and stiff at the age of 39 that if one of those guys had hit me I would have exploded all over the floor like a smashed vase.

Secondly, I wasn't sure about having some guy that close to me, scraping his legs, and undercarriage , and face, and knackers, and feet, and armpits that close to my body. At the age of 39, hadn't I earned the right to have at least some personal space in my life? It's bad enough having my kids try to get my attention in public by elbowing me in the gonads. So why should I pay some BJJ gym for the honour of getting steamrolled into oblivion by some other sweaty bloke? That wasn't my idea of a fun time.

Plus, again: feet. Oh man, in BJJ, it looked like there were so many bare feet involved. Feet don't look good on anyone, pretty much, I don't care what the sandal-makers tell us. Most people's feet tell their own brutal war stories on both men and women. Feet on kids are just cute little kids' feet. But once the hair starts sprouting, and our feet get trodden on, and fat, and the toenails get damaged, and they start to smell, and then we forget to clip the toenails and all that dirt gets caught under them, and then the nails turn yellow, and then the skin on the feet start to sag and wrinkle. And then they trap tiny balls of black sock between the toes… it's not pretty.

And never mind the weird lack of symmetry of most people's feet. And all of the above is basically just me describing my own feet.

So yes, all feet are a war zone in hell.

So to go to a Jiu-Jitsu club and have people sticking them in your face — granted, in order to rip your foot off the end of your leg — doesn't exactly seem as fun as doing all the other more pleasurable things you could be doing in that allotted slot of free time.

And that's before you even throw in the fact that this BJJ stuff is real. It meant that I'd actually be sparring. Because that's what they do. They fight each other all the time. There's none of this air-fighting tai-chi business. Everyone attacks each other with 100% force and enthusiasm. And I didn't know any of the moves.

I was scared.

Jiu-Jitsu to me seemed like a cauldron of smelly feet, the groins of strangers dangerously close to one's face, being contorted by other people like I'm a twistable balloon at a child's fifth birthday party, and the fact that I was now on the wrong side of the hill.

Plus, I was almost fifty percent through my lame life now already. And I'd survived, hadn't I, albeit in the face of some shocking physical confrontations I'd cowered at? Forget it, I reasoned. I'll just continue on as I always have done. I'll be fine!

And then, while cycling back home from work one evening,

inviting in lung cancer from all the vehicles I was sharing the busy roads and bus lanes with during rush hour, I got into yet another altercation.

I'd been cycling away up the hill, panting and pumping my fat little legs away as road grime slowly formed a film over my face — and then some bloke in a banger cut me up.

"Oy," I shout, my common retort, I now realise, when confronted by someone I think is trying it on.

In the middle of all these beeping horns and the chaos of rush hour, with all these working people just trying to get home to stick their pepperoni pizzas in the oven, the car I'd screamed "Oy" at stopped.

Oh, dear. My stomach began doing backflips because extreme nausea and trembling knees is how all war-ready soldiers are trained to respond, surely.

I kept cycling forwards. I passed him in his car, and he wasn't even eyeballing me. Instead he was doing that restless thing where you're just so immensely distressed when looking for a certain item that you've dropped in your car that your insane mind takes over. He was seeing red. Pure bloodlust. And he was looking for something in his car that could help him vent that fury on me. A sharp weapon? A bat? A giant foam Numero Uno hand with a finger pointing skywards like they have at American baseball matches? I didn't know. But it was serious. He wanted to kill me, 'The Rule of Law' be damned. "You know you'll end up on the wrong side of the law if you touch me," I wanted to mumble in a high-pitched bleat.

I got to the traffic lights ahead, at least twenty feet from his stationary car, although he'd actually just stopped in the middle of the road before the lights had turned red. He didn't give a damn, and in his red-misting mind, so what if the other cars had begun honking him, with frustrated Danny DeVito types leaning out of their taxi cabs and raising their arms in frustration. This guy was about to commit murder. And actually, the funny thing was, all my mind was saying, apart from the bit where I was panicking like mad and was wondering whether

I'd begun absentmindedly weeing a shape similar to the map of Africa down the front of the shorts I was wearing, was, "Wow, that really is one of the crappiest cars I've ever seen."

It was so dirty; an utter piece of rubbish. I know that's in keeping with the textbook idea of a serial killer who's flouted society's norms, and is more interested in eating his own mother's brain with a knife and fork than perhaps opting for the £25 foam and wax deal in his nearest hand car wash. But shouldn't he be venting that anger on his car instead, channelling that energy into fixing his utter £200 disaster on wheels?

How can you hate me when there's so much you could hate about your car?

Anyway, I also did genuinely think he had plans on murdering me and you don't stop Leatherface in his tracks as he's about to chainsaw you in half up from crotch to crown.

No, instead you snap out of your own daft inner chat and deal with the issue at hand: your own impending murder. So that's what I did.

So there I am, at the traffic lights, choking on car fumes, but also, now dipping my head into my shoulders like an embarrassed turtle, my penis also slowly retracting into my scrotum, mechanically, as penises seem to do in a crisis.

I get ready for the worst of this world.

And yet the crazy thing was, he just got out of his car, waved his arms, and screamed in some unidentifiable Poundshop Dolph Lundgren accent: "Next time I get you!"

That said, I have no doubt he would have just pummelled my fat face featureless, like a man's fist repeatedly hitting wet clay.

And I would have been effectively submissive to whatever he would have decided to do to me. It was an unsettling thought that lingered with me for, pretty much, not much longer than a week.

Why? Because a week later, I was again cycling home from work, this time on a sunny, still, late afternoon in the suburbs of London, when the terror I'd felt seven days earlier was ratcheted up further.

Like before, a fairly dilapidated car tore up beside me, so close in fact that like the last one, I was convinced it was about to hit me.

"Aaaah, WANKER!!!!" someone from the left side of the car shouted as it skimmed past me at speed.

"PISS OFF!" I shouted, suddenly, inexplicably, out of nowhere, not even realising that the words were coming out of my mouth.

The car slowed down. As in, 'Hollywood horror movie' slowed down.

Christ, I thought. There'd been more than one passenger in there; I might be in for a pasting here.

I'm 39, though, I reminded myself. Am I really going to get a skinhead-style battering? Aren't we all a bit past this?

The car did a slow, 180-degree turn and headed back down the hill towards me. There were no other cars about.

Why?

It was rush hour. What had happened? A zombie apocalypse? A secret World Cup?

Where the hell were my witnesses? Why wasn't there anyone here to help me?

The car drove closer until it was now three metres from me as my little chubby legs continued to pump up and down at the pedals, desperately.

There were four of them. They were emboldened by the number of them compared to just me on my bike. I could make that out from the aggressive, excitable body language of their silhouettes in the car.

Here it comes, I remember thinking. Oh God.

They were all rough-looking white guys, probably drunk, thinking about taking this situation up a gear. They liked the prospect of four men overpowering one with mindless, thoughtless, technique-bereft violence. They were thinking about pounding my skull in.

These lads felt the aura of their own dominating power.

And they fancied their chances. They were thinking of violence with impunity. Hurting another without witnesses or recourse. And I was to be their prey.

The car pulled even closer to me, at a prowl. There was a left-hand turning I could pull into, I saw; they were also about to pull into it, to directly cut me off.

I felt sick.

"I'll just keep throwing punches at them, like Dad would have told me to," I reminded myself, rattling any thoughts and experiences about fighting I may have had in my brain to the front of my mind, hoping that one new concept about how to defend myself might somehow apply in this situation. "Throwing punches like a madman, that should scare them off..."

And then I envisaged all four of them springing out of the car on this balmy summer evening and beating me within an inch of my life. I can't fight four people, I realised, they'd kill me.

And I wasn't about to punch them. We've all heard terrible stories of someone who hit someone else in a fight. And that person then fell backwards, banged his head on the pavement, and died from the effects of that kind of impact on his skull.

And frankly I didn't want to be the person who killed another man on the off-chance that he was going to beat me up. I didn't want that for them — even though they really did look like they were going to kill me. And I didn't want that for me. I didn't want to go to prison and have the freakish accidental death of another man on my conscience because my feelings had been hurt after he'd called me a tosser.

To punch someone in the face, I felt, would have to warrant someone having done something pretty awful to me or a loved one in my eyes.

So for now, until really pushed, I'd decided I'd be doing no punching of other people.

But as it looked like these four thugs were about to do me in, I stared at the meathead behind the steering wheel in the eyes. Not deep in the eyes, because through the reflection of the sun on the car's windscreen, I couldn't actually see him that well. But I stared at him, trying to work out what his next move might be.

Nevertheless, I don't know whether it was the fact that I was panting furiously up the hill and had a look of rigid determination on my face, or whether, because of the bright sun on the car's windscreen, I was squinting like Clint Eastwood walking out of the world's grimmest toilet.

But in that moment, I saw the eyes of a boy within the heavily-meated face of the man staring back at me.

I saw weakness. I saw humanity. I saw someone who had capitulated at the final moment. For all his bravado, he didn't have the heart to stop the car and kill me after all — even if his friends may have been a completely different kettle of fish.

And so I kept cycling past the car and up the hill. No one in that car said anything more to me, and I continued pedalling home furiously, wondering whether they'd now drive up behind me and car-barge me off my bike and possibly to my death.

But that little eye-to-eye standoff with the driver, through all my horrified fear, got me thinking: if I'd done like my dad had said back in the day to me, and just kept going forward, like the voice in my head also suggested, I would have been mullered by them; beaten to a pulp.

But I didn't try to take them on: I held back. I waited. Waited, actually, because I was terrified and was hoping for it to all go away. But when it didn't, and they looked into my eyes, they themselves weren't now sure how this one would play out.

Yes, they'd done all the aggressive turning around of their car. They'd committed to their aggression.

But when it came to the moment where they had to pull the trigger on me, they hadn't had the courage to do it. Why?

As I cycled up the hill towards home with sweat dripping into my eyes, I became convinced that they hadn't beaten me up because in this sweaty, exercise-enraged condition, I must have bizarrely looked like an unpredictable madman who could handle himself.

But in their misreading of my strained facial expressions — think: The World's Strongest Man after catching his willy in his jeans zip — they saw…confidence.

That's why the driver had bottled it when he looked into my eyes. He saw self-belief where there was none, and so the bully had backed off.

Which was exactly the attitude I'd always hoped to have had every single time I'd been started on by strangers in the street over the past 25-odd years.

Like I knew I had a little something special in my back pocket that I could use if the moment called for it.

So what could I do to always give off this aura, I wondered? I knew the answer, of course.

I knew what I had to do: I'd have to study Jiu-Jitsu.

Because the prospect of getting threatened as I got ever increasingly older and more frail was a future that was quite frankly giving me nightmares. If I wasn't able to defend myself throughout my teens, my twenties or my thirties, then what chance would I have if I was ever approached by a threatening person in middle or old age?

I remembered Mike Tyson once saying in an interview that when he was a kid he used to mug old ladies. And I didn't want to be prey to the bullies as I got older and even more vulnerable.

I'd even actually look at old people over 50 in the street and think, "If someone had bad intentions and wanted to beat you up and take your money, they could. And there'd be nothing you could do about it."

So I decided that I wasn't going to be one of those people — an open goal for muggers as I got older.

Jiu-Jitsu was going to be the form of self-defence that was going to keep me young.

Yes, I'd have to spar younger, stronger, more powerful guys. But being completely helpless when faced with the prospect of physical violence was something I no longer wanted to be haunted by.

And so I went online and looked for my nearest BJJ school.

Amazingly, I'd later learn that the Jiu-Jitsu academy only 15 minutes' drive from my house was in fact revered as one of the finest BJJ schools in the UK.

Not that I knew what a good and a bad BJJ school was at this stage.

Hyped up from continually listening to Jocko's claims on his podcast about how great Jiu-Jitsu is, though, I felt emboldened.

I picked an evening class to go to, and then prepared for it psychologically.

I was to fully commit to my BJJ journey. There was nowhere left to run.

CHAPTER FIVE

On a warm evening in September, I take the plunge.

Approaching the academy, its windows steamed thick with condensation, I take a deep breath and walk through the entrance.

The first thing that hits me is that the air is thick with sweat. You can feel its heaviness. At the same time, the gym itself doesn't appear to have that dangerous edge about it like an amateur boxing club does, where coaches and students are barking at each other, and the coach is shouting with fifty percent affection and fifty percent driven by the will to pull a bunch of long-suffering kids up by their bootstraps.

I think this is because boxing is a conveyor belt for young men from tough circumstances to learn about both discipline and having the strength to better oneself through the art of having a scrap.

Instead, at this BJJ gym, the vibe seems different. It isn't as outwardly aggressive. It does however feel like stepping into a new world. There's still a sense of violence in the air, but with less chest-beating.

In a boxing club, though, if you shout people still listen to you because no one knows how much damage you may or may not be able to inflict on everyone else if push came to shove.

With a BJJ gym, though, as I'd soon learn, there may be less posturing overall because your ability to fight is immediately on display by the colour of the belt you're wearing around your martial arts kimono. There are no belts at an amateur boxing club, so people judge you on your loud mouth and might take you at your word or your swagger that you can actually chainsaw through people in a fight.

But in Jiu-Jitsu, it turns out, there's no lying. If there's a small dweeb in the corner of the gym, with a black belt around his waist, that guy is an absolute killer. In a boxing gym, meanwhile, a big guy with few skills can still hurt a good little guy with some skill.

In BJJ, though, a big guy with few skills versus a small guy with good skills is a complete mismatch. The small guy would just scurry up the body of the big guy like a monkey, get round to his back and choke him out.

That's the beauty of BJJ. The moment you take leverage and distance away from a big guy, using BJJ — the moment you take it to the ground — the bigger, untrained guy is in serious trouble.

It's a fascinating thing to witness. There are no what-ifs and buts in a BJJ gym. Around your waist, with that belt, you're practically wearing a billboard that declares how well you'd do in an actual fight.

And so, the tendency is for athletes to stay humble, listen to the instructor and come to terms with the fact that when you're fighting someone of a higher belt, it's not a matter of 'if' he or she could finish you — but 'when'.

And that's another curious revelation that presents itself in Jiu-Jitsu. Watching everyone rolling around with each other on the mat as I walk through the gym, I see small-framed women contorting big men into submission.

I'm mesmerised by this fact. This sight alone is proof in action that Brazilian Jiu-Jitsu really is conceived in order to empower smaller framed people.

On the massive grey padded mat that takes up the majority of the floor space, around 20 guys of various builds and looks — some are are clean-shaven with tattoos, others wear elaborate or long facial hair — are rolling around on the ground, sweating all over and crushing each other under the heft of their respective weights.

Despite everyone seemingly attacking each other with everything they've got, no one appears to be panicking.

Just me.

I walk to the front desk and get handed a 'gi', which is basically a thickly woven kimono, like they wear in karate, only chunkier and more durable.

I get shown to the mat.

What follows is 30 minutes of an instructor demonstrating a technique that I'm to follow with a partner, despite the principles of the move completely going over my head. But it's at a nice pace. All is calm. Ok, I think. This isn't so bad. I've made it through. Sure, while practicing this move, I've had someone else's naked feet wafting past my nose and lips incessantly, which isn't a particularly pleasant experience. But whatever: I've survived!

"Ok, let's do some sparring!" announces the instructor.

A wave of nausea overcomes me. Sparring? As in, let's all fight now? I feel like I want to throw up, my stomach twisting in on itself tighter and tighter.

But I don't even know the rules, I'm thinking. What are the rules? Am I safe? Who'll save me if things get out of hand? Is anyone here reasonable?

The guy I'm told by the teacher to 'roll with' is a tightly muscled guy of medium height with a big, bushy beard.

But his smiling blue eyes intimate that underneath his human kindness, he means murder.

We slap our right hands with one another, then bump fists, as I'd soon learn is customary before each sparring session. And then it's ON.

Overcome by fear, and with the remnants of my old man's disproven advice to 'keep coming forward, no matter what', I go freaking 'loco down in Acapulco', and launch myself at him. It's what they call in this game (somewhat inappropriately — though I wasn't exactly going to get on my high horse about it), 'spazzing out.'

There I was, flailing around like a man possessed with both the devil and the spirit of comedian Robin Williams when he used to do all those funny voices in TV interviews, with all kinds of peculiar sounds coming out of my mouth.

But the funny thing is, that didn't help. I was trying to grab a hold of this smiling bearded man (who actually ended up being really nice about it at the end, and showing me where I was going wrong).

But it didn't help.

Obviously no punching or kicking is allowed, to my relief. And because I'd later learn that the sport is about cutting off the blood supply to your opponent's head or cranking their arm in a funny direction until they 'tap' you to let you know they've had enough, beyond that I had absolutely no tricks up my sleeve.

So I was just trying to strangle him while intermittently apologising because all the sweat from my bald head was going in his eyes. "That's fine," he'd say, stoically, before slowly and meticulously moving me around like a rag doll.

And then he turned on 'The Tap of Competence', and a sense of powerlessness overcame me, similar to how it might feel if you were picked up by the scruff of your neck by a marauding T-Rex.

Despite my desperate need to do Jocko proud, even though I've never actually met him, I suddenly experienced unbelievable fear, followed by utter self-disgust and shame.

As my bearded sparring partner wrapped his legs around me to control me at the hips so I couldn't move, he threw one of my wrists between his legs, pulled me by my other wrist towards him, and then wrapped both legs around the back of my shoulders.

Now, my right arm was flailing around on his chest, but my left arm was dangling around between his legs.

Unsettlingly, I now appeared to have my face stuffed deep into his undercarriage, breathing in and being asphyxiated by a complete lack of air. On the plus side, you can't even smell someone else's gut musk when you can't breathe at all.

Yet there was little time for reflection. I was going light-headed. The oxygen that would usually go to my brain was being choked out of me. I couldn't breathe.

And my own shoulder on the arm dangling through my opponent's legs and resting on his chest was restricting my airways even further.

I bucked and thrashed around and wriggled and moved about as much as I could but it only stifled my breathing further.

Jesus, I was going to pass out. I'd never been in this kind of situation before and it was terrifying.

Just to drive home the fact that I was totally at his mercy, he then got his left hand and placed it on the back of my head, pushing my face further into his body, taking me only seconds away from passing out.

As my body started to go limp from oxygen deprivation, I tapped twice on the right-hand side of the left leg of his that was helping to choke me.

And suddenly this this bearded killer relaxed his legs and the ability to breathe again came rushing back to me.

He'd caught me, I'd later learn, with a 'triangle', and it had nearly popped my head off.

And yet, I knew that both Jocko and 'fat me from when I was a kid getting beaten up' would have approved.

For once, I was being courageous. For once, I was fighting my fear with determination.

I'd just rolled with a guy who, if he hadn't let go of his triangulated legs around my neck after about two minutes, would have genuinely killed me.

I'd have been starved of oxygen to the brain and died.

So really, I owed this guy a debt of gratitude for not killing me.

I was to later discover that he was a highly regarded practitioner at the club — yet curiously, unlike other sports like amateur boxing where a good boxer isn't allowed anywhere near a bad boxer who's just started — in Jiu-Jitsu, everyone rolls with each other.

And usually after you've been made to tap about seven times within a six-minute sparring round, the guy you're rolling with will explain where you went wrong and what adjustments you could make to improve your game; a game where I had no clue what to do or how to do it.

But as I left that first class, my shoulders aching and feeling like they were about to pop off from having them contorted by subsequent sparring partners, I nevertheless felt elated. That had felt like I'd been in a real fight — I had been in a real fight! And I'd survived. I was thrilled.

CHAPTER SIX

As I kept continually going to classes after that, be it in gi, with the kimono on, or NOGI (where everyone just wears shorts and a t-shirt, and, less appealingly, everyone's covered in each other's sweat), I soon began to pick up a few moves. Even if trying to pull them off in the right sequence against a live opponent didn't always go too well.

"I've been training for 17 years," said the head instructor, a former world champion, to everyone at the end of class; his demeanour being a combination of charm and competence. "So, my approach has been to simply learn three techniques and perfect them each year. Over the past 17 years, then, that's 51 techniques that I have in my arsenal to call on at all times. So that's the way you should approach your training."

It was a fascinating idea — a real lightbulb moment for me — and the idea stuck.

From that point onwards, I decided, I too would try to master one new move every four months, starting with the very first technique that was used against me: the triangle!

But it was less easy than I imagined. For one, I kept forgetting to jam their head towards my hips whenever I had their one arm and neck between my legs.

Plus, all I wanted to say during sparring was, "Look, I'm so sorry, would you mind just not moving at all while I try to choke you?"

And, of course, that's never going to happen during sparring. They're also trying to choke you to out.

And then the inevitable happened: having spent the last few weeks staring at the misshapen cauliflower ears of everyone I sparred with at the gym, my right ear during one sparring round suddenly swelled up.

While trying to catch someone in a triangle, a sparring partner had smeared all 16-stone of his weight up my body, crushing the life out of me as he slowly but surely went towards my neck in order to sit his full weight on my chest.

And it was while whipping his left leg over my torso to pin me down under his weight that his knee banged against my ear.

My right ear felt simultaneously bruised and like it was on fire.

Once the session ended, as I changed and dressed for home in the changing rooms, I felt around the top of my ear.

It felt padded; swollen, like it had suddenly become all squishy. I didn't want anyone to notice my concern. I was embarrassed by my own pettiness. So, I quickly left and once in my car, I inspected the damage.

The top of my ear looked like it had been pumped full of custard.

After another 24 hours of examining my ear, the ear was now blackening at the top of it, like an old banana.

I'd thought it had just been some of the top instructors who had cauliflower ears. I thought they were something that took a lifetime of abrasion to earn.

But no, within my first month, my ears had already started to balloon. So now, I not only couldn't I fight — I also had ears that were becoming disfigured.

And the funny thing was that there were also white belts in the gym who had lumpy ears. And white belt isn't even a belt you actually earn in recognition of your improving skills.

No, in fact, white belt isn't actually a belt. Anyone can get one. And it takes up to two years or more to earn your blue belt, and then another two or more to earn your next one - the purple, before the brown and then the black, signifying roughly around a ten-year journey.

So here I was, with my white belt, that had none of the four stripes you intermittently earn on your way to the next belt up, and my ears were getting mashed.

Granted, many BJJ instructors' own ears tend to be cauliflower-ridden - and in the words of one, they were cool in that they were, in some sense, their own trophy, they told their own story.

But being a white belt with mangled ears? I wasn't so sure.

And so I went into a big panic attack. How many things had I done in my past that I'd never kept going with? Like skateboarding, drawing, running. You name it: I'd tried countless fads, and devoted huge portions of my life to them - and for what? To only give it up a few months or even a year or two later.

So what was to say that learning Jiu-Jitsu wouldn't be the same thing?

Only unlike rollerblading, I'd be permanently left with the results of my complete immersion into this fad. I'd be an old man eventually, with ears half-hanging and bent and twisted on the sides of my head from all that 'fad Jitsu'. What if I never even became good at it?

I'd be disfigured for life. And yet I'd have no credible fighting skills to show for it. I'd be like the old punch-drunk boxer who can barely string a sentence together and sounds like he's blowing raspberries when he speaks, but who'd also in fact just been an average boxer in his day. What would have been the point?

My fear was further reinforced by my GP when I went to see him about it. Scared that the blood that was filling a big blister in the top of my right ear would get bigger due to its continually getting rubbed on (and painfully so!) during Jiu-Jitsu, I'd gone for some advice.

In the lead-up to my appointment I'd also typed in 'BJJ cauliflower ear' into YouTube, and been horrified by the videos I'd seen.

There were some guys who'd gotten such bad cauliflower ear that it was the size of a golf ball. So to ease the pressure on the top of their bowing ears, they were asking their mates to lance their ears with a syringe and withdraw all the blood out of their newly formed ear bubbles so they'd go down.

And good Lord, the blood, pus and gunk that was being drawn away into those syringes was disgusting.

And yet the crazy thing was, these cauliflower ears were just refilling again as blood flowed back into these stretched pockets of skin at the tops of their ears.

So, to get some clarity on the issue, I found myself sat there timidly in front of my doctor.

And that's when my thoughts that maybe I shouldn't do this Jiu-Jitsu schtick after all really began to harden.

The doctor touched my right ear with his cold left hand, and he winced.

Admittedly, it wasn't the prettiest of sights. My right ear had now lost the normal shape it had previously had.

"How bad is it?" I ask. "Can you drain it?"

The doctor shook his head. "There's no way we can drain it now. You've left it too long to come and see me. The blood in there has congested and hardened. Generally, that's what happens if you leave it for more than a few days."

What? Oh, bloody hell.

"Anyway," he continued, "often draining cauliflower ears is pointless. If the skin has become detached from the ear in any way, blood will now just continue to fill it. So draining it would be a waste of time. I mean, I understand why you'd want to fix it…"

Thanks!

"…but if I were you I'd wait until you finally decide to stop doing Jiu-Jitsu. As it's going to keep happening. Even though it'll look horrible by the time you decide to give up your sport and fix your ear. I've seen some terrible-looking cauliflower ears in my time. Or you can hold off from doing Jiu-Jitsu for a few weeks and the blood will just drain back from your ear and into your body. So, yeah…"

Great. Those were my options: stop doing BJJ, for possibly three months, until my ear healed itself naturally. Or keep going to Jiu-Jitsu class, the aesthetics of my ears be damned.

Yet it was a decision that made itself. I'm an average looking guy, I'll be honest. Maybe the dodgy ears might give me some character, I reasoned.

Plus at middle age, and married for 7 years at this point, it wasn't like I was going to be trying to impress women. The only woman in my life was/is my wife, and she lost all respect for me from the moment she saw me naked (though probably went through with the marriage out of sympathy and a belief that having slept with me once, she'd be forever sullied anyway).

So forget it, I thought. I'm ugly. So are my ears. Fine. And actually, and most importantly, maybe my ears might even prove a deterrent from now on to potential aggressors I'd meet throughout life.

Maybe, like people with muscles who can just scare others and therefore be left alone by bullies on the basis of their threatening mass, maybe my half-gammy ear might detract people looking to beat me up, the next time that inevitably happened to me.

I'm sticking with Jiu-Jitsu, I reasoned. I needed to learn how to defend myself for real, not just in that way that chubby blokes do at weird balsa-wood karate-chopping exhibitions.

That said, I did decide to take precaution. Why have a golf ball on my ear full of blood if it wasn't necessary?

I tweeted Jocko Willink. "What would you recommend I do," I asked him.

"Get head gear," he replied, meaning the type of ear guards that American college wrestlers wear.

So that's what I did — to the hilarity of everyone I then sparred against at the academy.

Like, for example, the time in front of the whole class when the head instructor pretended to speak to me by mouthing words as if the ear guards were preventing me from hearing.

A week later though and I'm having an absolute breakthrough. Although I still have virtually no techniques to speak of, after being shown how to do a leg-lock — whereby you hook your opponent's ankle under your armpit and then turn away from their body until they tap in pain — the move suddenly gelled in my head.

Soon, I'd be sparring and the first thing I'd do was go for a leg-lock, often finishing it successfully. It was definitely progress.

All of a sudden, I had a thing. People were tapping to me, finally!

It was also for me a far less technical move than wrapping my legs around their neck and one shoulder to pull off the triangle. And I was able to get this move on people at least 80 per cent of the time.

I knew one chess move, basically!

But it felt great.

Plus I noticed that a lot of other people in the gym didn't tend to play leg-locks that much, not at this point in my journey anyway. The attitude seemed to be that you only go for leg locks when you can't control their body and do Jiu-Jitsu properly. Which was true. I was testament to that.

"Just be careful when you do them," one of the instructors told me.

I nodded.

Okay, no problem. But why?

"Otherwise you're reaping."

I tried to understand what reaping was. "It's when your foot on their hip slips down to their leg."

"And is that not allowed?" I asked.

"No, it's against the rules of the International Brazilian Jiu-Jitsu Federation."

Ok, fair enough, I thought. I don't want to break the rules. So I must watch that my legs don't slide down in front of my opponents.

But then I left it at that — a huge mistake on my part that would soon come back to haunt me. I didn't understand that what I was really being told was: you're running the risk of your ankle bending your opponent's knee back on itself.

And so I ploughed on, mindful not to reap.

Nevertheless at least I had one little superpower that I now had the option to unleash. And that felt great.

And so I looked up the training videos of Jocko's training partner Dean Lister, a famous BJJ fighter and instructor from San Diego who is famed for his technical leg submissions.

I went with my leg-lock journey.

Until the day, that is, that I caused an almighty stink in the gym that I'd soon realise was entirely my own fault.

CHAPTER SEVEN

It was during sparring in a lunchtime class, while rolling on the mat with another white belt, that I started doing Dean Lister's various leg attacks that I'd learnt via YouTube.

I grabbed his leg, stepped sideways, hugged his foot as I fell back then thrust my hips forward to produce just enough pain that my opponent would tap.

One of the instructors was pointing at me, talking about me to another instructor.

They must be discussing how much I've improved, I reasoned.

(Actually, absolutely not as it soon turns out).

My opponent tapped again.

But then he stood up and walked to the other side of the class. In the middle of the sparring round. Just as I was trying to work out why he'd just walked away from me, the buzzer to signify the end of the round went off.

I walked over to him and stood next to him by the wall where everyone in the class was lining up to get paired off for the next sparring round.

"Everything ok?" I asked.

"Yeah. I'm fine."

But he looked cross. And I was disturbed that I'd made someone feel like this. I didn't understand why he was so shaken up, and that had shaken me up because it'd brought up in me all these shameful feelings about how I'd been made to feel by aggressors throughout my life, and how, in some way, even though we were operating within the rules of Jiu-Jitsu, I'd now had some hand in making my fellow white belt feel a mixture of anger and fear.

I was overcome by feelings in both my stomach and my mind that I could barely understand.

The instructor gathers the class and tells us briefly about the various things we were all doing in sparring; where we could have done things better with our technique, and things we were doing that he was encouraged by.

And then he came out with it:

"...And if I see any white belts doing knee-bars again on people, then they can train at another gym! I won't tolerate that kind of behaviour here."

I was mortified. I didn't even know what a knee-bar was but I knew in that instant that the instructor was talking about me, because there were only four other white belts in the class.

Plus I had really, genuinely upset that other white belt, and so my instructor's anger was bound in with my fellow white belt's anger and fear and disgust with me during our spar.

It's a reaction from both of them that I now know was totally reasonable.

"It was me," I said, thinking that honesty was the best tactic, even though I didn't really understand what my crime was.

"I know it was you," the instructor said, and actually if I'd have been him, and had seen that, knowing what I know now, I'd probably have said something to me far worse.

At the end of the class, I approached him to talk through what I'd done wrong so I can get a better handle on it, but he wasn't not interested.

He turned his back to me and walked off, shaking his head in anger and disappointment.

I tried to apologise profusely, saying that I knew ignorance wasn't a defence, but I really wasn't sure what I'd done. I was guilty of committing an offensive act, it seemed, but I didn't feel guilty in my mind — mainly because I still didn't under-stand the rules and risks of the sport.

'Why were those moves the cause of so much consternation on his part?' I'd later reflect.

But he wasn't having any of it. He wouldn't even respond to my queries.

I was horrified. Only now do I realise that my instructor was absolutely right.

I'd later learn that a knee bar is something only brown and black belts are allowed to do.

Why? Because a knee bar, where you place your hips on your opponent's knee and bend it back in a direction the knee isn't happy with, places such unbearable pressure on the knee cap that it can cause the victim immense damage. So the idea is that you are only allowed to apply it on people when you know when to pull back a little in order that you don't cause your sparring partner permanent knee damage.

Which makes sense thinking about it now, but at that point I just thought a knee-bar would cause my opponent a fraction of pain similar to that of a leg lock and then he'd tap.

But I was wrong. With use or receive knees bars,you need to be advanced enough to know how to either move out of its way, or tap immediately once the pain is on, saving yourself vast amounts of knee pain by trying to wriggle out of it the wrong way.

So a brown belt doing it to a brown belt is fair game. They both know how to defend it because they've learnt the defensive moves. Plus a brown belt is experienced enough to know that you actually feel the pain of a knee-bar way after it's actually started to cause your knee damage (something I'd later learn after someone did one on me).

They really are awful things, knee-bars, because the moment you know your knee is in pain, your knee is already 20 percent ruined.

But I didn't know this then. I didn't take the time to actually learn about the rules surrounding knee-bars. I completely failed in my bid to understand what I should and shouldn't do while sparring. Especially for a white belt.

So a white belt like me with no skills doing it to another white belt with equally few skills was a serious no-no. It's effectively one idiot causing an innocent untrained person potentially irreparable harm. All of which became apparent to me as I looked into it, and was overcome by a sense of horror.

And it's that level of naivety on my part as a white belt that explains why, in some Jiu-Jitsu gyms, there's generally a view that white belts are a joke. That they aren't worth much. That they should just shut up, stop talking, stop showing off pretending they know anything, and just get the stuffing beaten out of them without any complaints.

And actually although I was initially offended by this, I soon began to see why this attitude towards white belts develops.

Most white belts after a fair few sessions can't, I think, believe they've survived having multiple versions of the closest thing you might get to an all-out fight on the street. In one sparring class you've effectively had an all-out fight with around six different people, all of various shapes, speeds and sizes. All of them going at you full pelt. And somehow you lived to tell the tale.

Yes, Jiu-Jitsu may have no kicking and punching in it. But then it's basically anything goes (eye gouging, slaps, kicks, fisticuffs — and definitely knee bars aside). So the endorphin flood of relief between classmates in the changing rooms after sparring is palpable.

But when you first start, you're just going absolutely bonkers fighting another man.

When I'd started I'd use every last bit of energy I had trying to dominate my opponent, which exhausted me, and then, now knackered, I'd get the life crushed out of me, which would make me flail about even more, inducing further exhaustion and panic. And then, as usual, I'd get choked out.

But because I kept getting tapped, I'd keep going even harder. Which saw me get tapped out even more. It took me — like many white belts — a very long time to realise that success in BJJ is about using technique, not using physical strength, even though I'd heard instructors say this relentlessly.

Consequently in my daft bullheadedness, I would flail around like a madman, with none of the self-control, thinking, and calmness I'd see in the other belts as they submitted their opponents.

So I'd just 'spaz out', as it's called in Jiu-Jitsu. And it would never, ever work. I'd push people off my chest and get my arm bent back on itself in an arm-bar or have someone wrap themselves around my back and choke me. It was terrible.

However there's an upside to this. Eventually the white belt wises up to this, stops flailing about, remembers how to pull off one technique finally, and begins to occasionally tap the newer students who join the academy after him.

And then, with those two submissions under his belt, if he's not careful, he begins to think he's The Man.

A swagger follows even though he's just a white belt — "a lousy white belt," goes the timeworn joke by some at the academy above him. And then the dark side takes over and he starts to convince himself that he's actually good at fighting, instead of thinking what the truth is. Which is: "Oh, look. That one single Jiu-Jitsu technique I've learnt works after all.

But no. Instead some white belts begin to think they're now bringing something unique to the sport. When you know nothing though, you have very little concept of how very little you know.

If you're a white belt, compared to a black belt who himself considers he's still learning, and has been playing the sport for at least ten years, then yes, absolutely. A white belt knows nothing.

You see this at work all the time too: the arrogance of carrying out one or two decent jobs soon completely enveloping a young guy in the company until his inevitable hubristic fall from grace. Beginners in any game — from Jiu-Jitsu to the professional world — don't understand that it's a marathon, not a sprint. And that you will eventually get your arse handed to you multiple times, and in the same way that the young gun soon gets tapped, so too does the king at the top of the hill. The similarity between the king and the fledgling hero is that both are soon inevitably brainwashed by their own arrogance.

And so they get smashed or toppled. There is always someone out there who can tap you out.

And in the context of Jiu-Jitsu, it's like an 8-year-old child scoring a few goals on a football pitch for his school team and suddenly thinking he's Cristiano Ronaldo.

To be really good at your sport or your professional field, you have to 'play' it for at least 20 years. And you have to have given it your all, non-stop.

Of course you do. Otherwise all the professional athletes whose actions we wow over would be little snot-nosed turds running around on a football pitch.

But that's not how it works. And actually to become good at a sport, it's inherent that you've therefore spent an awfully lengthy amount of time being fairly crap at it.

But you stick with it. And that's how it is with Jiu-Jitsu. It takes years and years and years to be half-decent.

What's more, it actually takes ages for one's traditionally up-right and fairly fragile body to adapt to both the movements and the ability to fight while in those types of positions. Your body over time adjusts to the idea of you hanging upside down off someone's waist while still attacking them. It takes time.

It also takes a long while for the mind to adjust to all the thinking you have to do while attacking or defending yourself from an opponent - or doing both simultaneously.

There's a huge amount to think about from getting them to the ground, to controlling them with your own body, to transitioning to a position where you can put a lock or choke on them, and then finally pulling off the move so that they tap. There are so many details to remember. And this all happens while your opponent is either trying to escape or actually trick you into committing to a move that he or she can then counter as part of their own attack. It really is cerebral work.

But because the average adult white belt has spent years not getting into fights, or hasn't been in fights because we live in a reasonable society where getting into fights can often lead to jail time as well as (thankfully) in many cases a fairly large dose of regret, the moment you survive a few sparring sessions at your local Jiu-Jitsu school, you think you've suddenly become the street fighting wizard you always dreamt of becoming.

But of course it's not that simple.

And I think that's why there's so much eye-rolling when people mention white belts. The less they know, the more mindlessly aggressive they can be in sparring.

They often won't let their sparring partners do any technical practice because they're flailing about wildly and going loco down in Acapulco.

Instead they're tempted to turn it into a strength contest, especially if they're big meatheads. And then people who want to practice their Jiu-Jitsu find themselves trapped in death matches when all they want to do is flow around on the mats.

Ironically, though, as a white belt imbued by a new identity as someone who fights at the academy a lot, there's the temptation to think that you know it all.

It's only after repeatedly going to classes over months and months that you think, "Wow, I actually know zero."

It was in fact actually quite amazing how little I knew as a white belt after nearly three years of going three times a week — arguably the same amount of time the average student puts into their university degrees.

Often as a white belt, meanwhile. you'll be making some good progress and thinking, "Hmm, I think I'm getting the hang of this," and then while sparring someone — or a series of consecutive sparring partners — they'll roll through you like you a tank driving through a pile of leaves. Like you're a limp, massive novelty teddy bear and they're just manipulating your body as they like.

What I do know is that they weren't thinking about the threat my Jiu-Jitsu posed them at all. They've seen every single thing I could think to do against them and so they'd just me you absentmindedly like they're putting out the bins on Tuesday night for the following morning's collection.

And then move on to the next sparring partner to tap.

So for a white belt like me at this stage to pretend that he's in any way a threat to a more advanced level would have been ludicrous.

However after my instructor quite rightly blew his lid for the fact I'd knee-barred someone, and I didn't really understand why he'd gotten angry with me, I started looking everywhere for answers.

Maybe it was because I'd been one of those cocky white belts I'd just described. That was possible, I reasoned.

But there was another reason why he might be angry with me, suggested the thoughts that began clattering around my mind. Maybe he thinks I'm a 'creonte'.

In BJJ lexicon, a creonte is someone who trains at one gym, absorbs as much as he can from one instructor, and then takes all that knowledge, and then moves to another academy, thereby stealing his instructor's investment in him and betraying his former teacher's trust.

In BJJ, until fairly recently after it became such a huge global sport, a creonte was and in some parts still is seen as the worst kind of vermin ever - yes, even worse than a cocky white belt.

And I can totally sympathise with this way of viewing such an apparent act of betrayal.

A teacher spends all that time pouring his hard-earned tricks into your mind so that the bar of excellence is raised at the academy through which your instructor quite rightly defines himself, and then you move on to train somewhere else.

The flip side to this argument, and I do think it's a credible one, is that with so many clubs widely available in many big towns and cities, BJJ enthusiasts who work full-time or travel a lot for their work might want to take advantage of a BJJ gym right next to where they're currently staying as it's the only chance they'll have to squeeze in some sparring and learning around their busy work schedule or family duties.

Other mitigation in the face of a creonte accusation is that everyone is on their own unique BJJ journey and if they want to pay to go to another gym as well in order to max out how many hours of Jiu-Jitsu they can squeeze into their week, then fair play to them. This was the argument I held onto nervously as I flitted between my home academy and one a few doors down the road near work. The academy was my base, but the gym near work was a bonus.

Plus, as I weakly tried to comfort myself, a gym is a business and if you want to pay for a service, and a gym is happy to accept your money in order for you to train there, then why should that be a problem?

Or so the various theories go.

And yet, I was guilty of being a creonte at two other gyms (one of which was affiliated with my gym) because of how much I travelled around on work.

Which would have mortified some instructors.

Yet soon I stopped training at that non-affiliated academy altogether. Why?

Because going there made me understand the definition and terrifying power of personality cults.

CHAPTER EIGHT

This non-affiliated gym in particular was completely bonkers.

Desperate to fit in a training session next to a work location I was briefly based at, I nipped through its doors. I was now in love with Jiu-Jitsu. At this gym, Jiu-Jitsu was their lives. What could go wrong?

I paid my one-off training fee. And because I was slightly late, I quickly threw on my gi, and headed to the mats.

The class had started, to my horror. Students were running around the mat in a circular motion to warm up, like they also do at my home gym.

And so, having been told five minutes earlier by the receptionist to join the class, I head to the end of the queue of students and start jogging.

"Hey you?"

My stomach drops.

"Yes?"

I'm hailed over by the class' enraged instructor who's also the club owner, a black belt with a beard and a massive chip on his shoulder.

"Do I look like a clown?" he shouts in my face.

Blimey, this guy is furious. I've run onto the mats with all the self-enforced innocence of an apologetic 8-year-old who's late for his exam. I made a distinct promise to myself, as I did at my home academy, not to impose my personality onto anyone. When you're a white belt, you maintain a respectful silence. No one wants a white belt to bleat on about their life. Be respectful, I told myself. Wind your neck in. You're here to learn. And so, for the first two years at my home academy, I distinctly just went about my business listening, learning, and not trying to blabber on.

Nevertheless, right now in this gym, I could tell I was under attack almost immediately, and I hadn't even opened my mouth.

"I said, 'Do I look like a clown to you?'"

He looks down at my white belt, with its paltry two stripes on, that highlight that I'm not just from another gym, but also that I'm a know-nothing white belt.

"I-I-I'm sorry but I don't know what — "

"Look at my face!" His eyes are wide with intense fury now.

Through my peripheral view and hearing, I can sense that the whole class has stopped jogging to watch what's happening in front of them with their instructor and I, this 'foreign invader' from another club who just paid his £15 to train here.

And then I think, "Hold on… He's re-enacting the 'Goodfellas'-Joe Pesci scene on me; that iconic moment in the film where Henry Hill, the film's main character, laughs at one of Pesci's jokes, then mutters, "You're funny…"

At which point, Pesci's face drops, and he says, "What do you mean, 'I'm funny.' Funny, how? Like a clown?"

Following which, Henry Hill, no pushover himself, recoils in horror, and goes into extreme apology mode, knowing Pesci's volcanic temper and easiness with committing acts of hard-core violence on others.

Now, as pop culture goes, if you suspend all sense of morals and truth, it's a cool scene, because it's a great bit of filmmaking. And we'd all hate to be Pesci's victim in that instance.

HOWEVER. That's in the movies. That's a slice of Hollywood. What on Earth is this instructor doing imitating Joe Pesci, and doing it with conviction, as if I don't know the reference, in order to intimidate and embarrass me? I'd been three minutes late to his class. 'I understand that you may be upset about this,' I'm thinking, 'and I'm truly sorry. My goal was never to disrespect you.'

But in the real world, there's a thing called proportion, as well as common reason and balance, where your reaction should only be in proportion to my alleged crime, instead of shouting in my face, bellowing, "DO I LOOK LIKE A CLOWN?"

How about I bleat, "Luke, I am your father," and we just leave it at that? 'No, Mr. Bond — I expect you to die!'

Or shall I just give it a sec while you go through Empire.com's list of The 100 Best Films of All Time, shouting in my face things like, "Say 'what' again! I dare you. I double dare you!!' And, "I LOVE THE SMELL OF NAPALM IN THE MORNING!" even though we're really in a beginner's Jiu-Jitsu class for white belts. I mean, really.

It was ridiculous. Mate, just have a word with me for being late. I'm genuinely sorry.

And so, to counter this bully, I decided to use what I'd learnt so far about the mind from Jiu-Jitsu — but on him.
'Actually, do you know what, pal?' I remember thinking. "You're a black belt, yes, and you may be the king in here, but if you want to play mind games with me, then I will rise above you psychologically in the same way that you can cook me out on the mats.' In the words of Michelle Obama, "When they go low, we go high."

Basically: 'damn you for trying to bully me so that you can power up your own ego bank.'

Because as he was shouting in my face and putting on such a huge performance for his students to see, what he was really doing was singling me out for humiliation. And in here, he believed, I would have no recourse. The entire academy had been built in his honour, pictures of him on the walls, the character of the place set in plaster by years of his inappropriate behaviour.

And having been intimidated plenty of times by now in my everyday life, Jiu-Jitsu had taught me that even at my inexperienced level, you never fight your opponent's fight. Sure, he had Jiu-Jitsu up his sleeve, but I had common decency and The Rule of Law.

In Jiu-Jitsu, I was learning that if they're bigger than you, don't try to out-muscle them. Use speed to your advantage instead.

Likewise, if they're bullying you like this guy was with his intimidating, overshadowing threat of violence, the cleverest thing you can do is turn your brains on and out-think him.

So that's what I did here.

Because if this cretin by anyone's standards was going to use power and hierarchy to intimidate me, then I was going to humiliate him back by using the only fighting trick I had in my back pocket: very good manners.

His behaviour seemed so nonsensical, you see, so contrived, that the only way of not getting crushed into an emotional wreck was by relying on my part of the social contract — which is common courtesy, the kind of human decency that elevates us above mindless beasts.

And so, through good manners, I slowed the fight down, in the way Jiu-Jitsu black belts do on the mat, and decided that I'd only move when I'd secured the position on my opponent.

"Does this look like a circus to you?" he continued. "DOES IT?"

"Erm…"

"DOES THIS LOOK LIKE A CIRCUS?"

I was tempted to reply, "Does. Marcellus. Wallis. Look. Like a bitch!'

I didn't.

I paused my body language, and gave him nothing back. I know that anything I say will be twisted and shouted back at me.

Reinforcing my confusion however is my ignorant belief that everyone who does Jiu-Jitsu is fundamentally a good person, because all I've encountered through the sport so far are good, positive people, in spite of them all trying to crush and choke me out.

But this guy, I realised, was the exception to the rule. And why not? Not all humans are good, just like not all people that do BJJ are good.

And there was proof of it in other gyms too. Jiu-Jitsu might be a force for good, but that doesn't mean that everyone who likes and uses it is fundamentally a good person. Far from it sometimes.

I spoke to one black belt recently who came to my home academy for a few sessions who explained that he'd left his gym because there was a purple belt there who was intentionally hurting people in training.

And the only reason this purple belt wasn't kicked out of that gym was because he was one of their best fighters.

And this was a black belt who was fleeing his own home gym, even though a black belt has often trained for at least ten years; double the time of some purple belts.

Which is obviously absolutely abhorrent. In my gym, I got scolded for using knee-bars, my claims of ignorance quite rightly be damned.

But to be a higher level belt and to be intentionally causing people physical damage? That's crazy. More so given that even this black belt was afraid of getting hurt by some lunatic.

So yes, I was beginning to understand. Jiu-Jitsu, like any sport or interest, is just human nature channelled into a certain activity.

This purple belt had been a lunatic.

And now stood before this black belt instructor right now in this new club I was visiting, here too was an example that although BJJ is a wonderful gift to the world, not everyone can be entrusted to wield its power. If power is said to corrupt, then in the case of this knob head with a black belt around his waist, owning his own gym had completely corrupted him.

As much as my arriving a minute or two late may have caused offence, nothing warranted him shouting in my white belt face. I was a beginner. I was paying to use his gym. I was a customer.

I hurried onto the mats to join the others jogging because I thought that that was the polite thing to do.

Anyway, instead of completely flapping with panic, I remembered all the terror that that bully in the train station passageway had caused me. I remembered the fear I'd felt while cycling home that summer afternoon when that car full of skinheads had turned around at the top of the hill and driven back towards me.

And so, slowly, I looked this preposterous Joe Pesci-wannabe in the eye, and said: "I'm so sorry. I meant you no disrespect. Can you please explain to me what I've done wrong?"

He gauged my body language, but also my lack of fear, bolstered by my own self-belief in what constitutes reasonable behaviour outside of these four gym walls; the fact that I wasn't prepared to humble myself beneath the bar of human standards in order to beg for his acceptance into this personality cult where everyone obeyed his commands on the promise of hopefully getting that next belt up around their waists.

In life, when you value something, and you're trying your hardest, and you're making progress, it feels wonderful to be acknowledged for your efforts. Especially if, like in Jiu-Jitsu, improvements don't come fast. In this sport, you really do have to earn those stripes around your belt.

Yes, a stripe is just a small strip of protective finger tape that's wrapped around your smelly belt by your proud teacher. Each belt meanwhile is said to symbolically represent the various shades your initially bright white belt goes through as it gets dirtier and dirtier on its way to black. And you don't make it to the next belt until you've genuinely earned those four stripes. And you really do have to have improved markedly between each stripe to get your latest one.

So that's why being given a stripe at the end of a Jiu-Jitsu class feels like such a big event.

But because you want a stripe, you also look out for the approval of your coach. And that means there's a temptation to idolise him or her. They're obviously the gatekeeper between who you are and who you hope to become.

And so, in the case of this bullying black who was currently terrorising me, you end up with a scenario where a guy who in the real world may carry no celebrated currency (because he's not advancing society in any way beyond his own self-indulgence), suddenly gets elevated to the role of a king by his students.

Nevertheless, I wasn't having any of this if it meant losing all self-respect and letting this plonker harangue me. If you've started shouting in the faces of your visitors for some alleged slight without even explaining the slight in question, in my mind you lose all credibility.

His thinking though seemed to be, "I don't need to be respectful because I outrank everyone here."

Which was an attitude I couldn't abide. And so, I took his aggressive approach and decided to give him enough rope to hang himself, so to speak, just like a good old-school journalist might do to a subject who's being unbearably arrogant.

"I'm so sorry, I don't understand," I said, doing my best 'pretending-to-be-patient' Louis Theroux impression. "Why would I think you look like a clown?"

"Because..." he paused. His mind kicked in again. "Does this look like a circus?"

It was a yes or no answer but I wasn't going to play his game. There was no chance on Earth I was going to give him an 'in', an opening, to destroy me.

"I'm so sorry, I don't understand what you mean?"

"DO I LOOK LIKE A CLOWN?"

"I don't understand."

I looked at him for an explanation.

He was now so exasperated that he couldn't really explain his metaphor to the students he was performing for. Instead just pointed me towards the mat, and I joined the class.

During the class, the madness continued.

"Who am I?" he shouted at his students out of nowhere, looking for validation.

"Our bright, shining star!" this big white belt chanted back.

The insane shouty black belt smiled with deep satisfaction. "Blooming hell," I remember thinking. "In martial arts movies, this would definitely be the baddies' dojo." The man was an egomaniac.

And although I went up to him at the end of the class to apologise further, to smooth things over, he just wasn't interested. The moment had moved on, the audience had dissipated, and in fact it appeared that the entire fiasco was never really about my alleged indiscretion at all.

Instead it appeared to be opportunism on his part. He'd had an audience when he'd scolded me. He'd been given the chance to shout at a white belt in me who he knew couldn't beat him in a fight.

So, like all bullies, he'd taken the chance to plug into me and boost his batteries. And I was paying financially for the privilege when I walked in and handed over my one-off session fee.

As I left the club I vowed never to go back.

CHAPTER NINE

When I told some of the high-level students at my home club about this episode, however, they all laughed. It turned out that this abusive black belt was notorious for his unpleasant disposition.

Countless students, it turns out, had left his club in the past and joined others, complaining about this bloke.

And that's really what he was: just a bloke. The fact he had a black belt around his waist didn't mean that students should preclude an expectation of common courtesy from others. "Sure, he's a really horrible guy, but hey, he's experienced at doing this thing that only a niche community cares about," isn't an acceptable excuse.

It seemed that the higher the standard of a club's fighters, and the more celebrated its medal-winning team, the more relaxed they were with their students. The absolute axe-wielding killers on the mat were often the most chilled. Probably because when you're a superman and you can turn on the murder tap at any time you like, and you know you can seek, smash, and destroy someone in a fight with a second's notice, one tends to be more Zen. You wield power more responsibly. You've tested yourself repeatedly. So you aren't like a yapping Jack Russell dog vying for everyone's attention. You've been there, you've done it. So they were laid back.

They knew they could — so they didn't have to.

Nevertheless, that's not to say that this event didn't completely throw me for a loop. After one of the instructors at my own home club had berated me for doing knee-bars on fellow students, and then this total lunatic at that gym I'd visited had euphemistically ripped by gonads off for being late to his class, I did pause for thought.

Maybe I was the problem. Maybe the reason two black belts

had shouted at me was because I needed to be shouted at.

After all, as much as that black belt from that other club had been a total plonker, I had been late for his class.

Yes, he'd overreacted and taken an opportunity to single me out in order to boost his own self-esteem. But I had been in the wrong. I'd been late. Plonker or no plonker, I had been at fault, no matter how apologetic I was.

And at my own club, I had intentionally tried to knee-bar other white belts. I had done that. There was no denying it. That was also wrong of me. I was also, in the strictest sense, a 'creonte', because I trained at more than one gym.

Yet for all these negative thoughts, there was just one prevailing thought: to just keep my head down and keep training. Like in Jiu-Jitsu, when someone has you in a very precarious position and your nerves start flapping and your mind starts racing, in my case thinking, "Am I about to be suffocated to death by this human mattress on top of me?", the worst thing you can do is let panic cloud your mind, like black ink seeping through water.

Instead, as I was learning, you need to think, "What's the most technical thing I can do right now, in this exact position, at this exact moment?"

And so that's what you do, whether it's an emotional life problem or while you're doing Jiu-Jitsu. No more flapping. No more panic. No self-exhausting thrashing about. Jiu-Jitsu is really a battle of the minds, with your body doing your mind's bidding.

You still your thoughts, block out the nervous self-chatter and do just that: try to get out of this funk at that exact moment doing the most technical thing possible you can think of.

So that's what I did here.

Which is this case meant focusing more on training. I threw my mind even further into understanding the sport. I kept my mouth shut, I opened my ears more, and I got stuck in.

My thinking was that the more I showed up, the more the positives would outweigh the negatives. And it worked.

Soon both incidents were behind me.

I was now training every day.

I'd moved on.

And the more I trained, the more I could practice how to guillotine, triangle and choke my opponents.

And soon those earlier concerns began to disappear from my mind.

Granted, on the mats, I was still getting submitted loads, but I was also getting far better at, at the very least, anticipating what my better opponents were trying to do to me, and then sort-of countering their moves so they wouldn't be able to tap me that easily.

And soon, although I was right at the bottom of the pyramid at my gym, on the street I felt a lot more confident and it certainly felt like I was giving off an aura that I could handle myself better.

To my shame, though, this then meant that when I was drunk at a friend's house, and I'd mention Jiu-Jitsu, or even think about it, all I'd want to do is to do it. And so, what would have started off as a pleasant, middle-class dinner party on a balmy summer's evening among a few old friends would end up with me tragically trying to wrestle my equally ageing mates among coffee table and chairs as books and magazines would be knocked to the floor.

And although I'm supposed to be really ashamed about this, mainly because I virtually knew no Jiu-Jitsu, just thinking about it is actually bringing a smile to my face.

Because it was just so much fun. And what would be so telling is that once I'd wrap my legs around people, they wouldn't have the foggiest what to do. They'd sort of just throw their bodies onto me.

And that's right: why should they know what to do. We weren't doing BJJ, we were having a play fight.

But like myself when I started Jiu-Jitsu, once the fight actually begins and the talking is done, very few people actually know what to do next.

And so they sort of just flop around above you like a dry fish.

Which is exactly what rolling in Jiu-Jitsu starts to feel like when you've done it for about a year and a new white belt rolls with you.

They have no idea what's happening to them, let alone any clue that they're being physically manoeuvred into a position that may not go well for them.

Equally revealing for me, though, was that over time, I was no longer the worst person — the newest white belt — on the mat, which blew my mind.

You also find yourself not going in as hard with new white belts even though they're going hell for leather on you, because you still remember what it was like when you were in their position: they just have very little sense of what controlling their opponent entails.

As I slowly got better, I also realised that the best thing to do if a white belt has just started is to put yourself in the worst position possible for you, preferably without letting them know so as not to insult them, and then just trying to work on your escapes. Because, really, do either of you learn if you're tapping him for the sake of it over and over and over? I don't think that really helps anyone.

Except that this, embarrassingly, wasn't what I'd be thinking when I'd be play-fighting with my oldest mates from school on nights out. I'd enjoy myself and go for it.

And I am ashamed to admit that, as we were thrashing around in a friend's back garden, sometimes it did get out of hand, to the extent that on one occasion my friend's wife came outside, winced at myself and a friend rolling around in the grass, and had to ask us to please stop. We all shot up from the garden grass and started apologising.

She was right: there are few things more pathetic than a bunch of 40-year-olds play-fighting.

Yet all of us enjoyed it, even those among us who weren't normally aggressive. And I think that's because deep down all men in one way or another love to fight, and if they don't have the skills to do it physically, then they'll rely on having a mental edge.

And yet play-fighting with my friends was very different from actually fighting either someone who knows what they're doing or some stranger just coming for you in the street.

If I really wanted to test my newfound skills, however, I'd actually have to fight someone who wanted to destroy me. That's how I'd know whether I'd earned the right to feel confident.

And so, feeling nervous, I decided to do it.

I decided to sign up for a Jiu-Jitsu fight.

After all, winning in a fight, I was realising, even at my rubbish level, isn't just about "throwing punches and just coming forward and never taking a step back," as my Dad had told me in a foreshadowing of the absolute battering I'd subsequently get as a youngster by heeding his advice.

Instead, success in battle is about attacking as well as withdrawing. You don't just go in a straight line, but instead you attack your opponent where he's weakest. You work around the problem. If someone is stronger than you at doing something, you shouldn't attack them head-on and play their game. You need to find a 'side door' to their weaknesses and attack them that way.

This would be my key learning going into a BJJ fight, I told myself. I'd use my brain instead.

And so, although I knew that if I entered a tournament I'd get totally Hulk-smashed, I felt compelled to take the leap. How could I take myself on this journey of self-defence, to take comfort in the ability that I could now possibly protect myself in a street fight, if I was still too terrified to actually have a fight? It was simple: I needed to compete. To see how this form of fighting actually works when someone who you haven't built a strong relationship with at your gym is coming at you and trying to rip your head off.

There was no way to avoid it. It was time to sign up to a tournament, and I could feel myself being drawn towards the prospect of competing.

Once I'd made the decision, once I'd had the epiphany, I was in, and that was it.

And so I began to watch videos of BJJ fights on YouTube — and felt consumed by terror.

CHAPTER TEN

In competitions, people looked vicious. So aggressive. So strong. Like they really planned to do some damage. What if a rival broke my neck or ripped my kneecap off and I was no longer able to walk?

As I watched these videos of one huge sweaty bloke stinking of sweat-and-cheesy-feet submitting another, all I could think was how competent and technical most fighters looked in tournaments. I only had two stripes on my white belt. TWO STRIPES! In Jiu-Jitsu terms, I was a one-year-old. A nobody. I had no BJJ thoughts in my head of any worth. I was a child. And even though I'd be fighting other white belts, there was a huge difference between my competence level and a white belt with four stripes. And yet this is who I'd possibly be up against.

There's even quite a gulf meanwhile between a one-stripe white belt and a two-stripe white belt, daft as that sounds.

So the gulf between me and some of my opponents would be humongous. Which meant I'd be stepping far outside of my comfort zone in any national BJJ competition.

And yet I knew that this was something that I had to do. I had to step into the lion's cage.

Looking at all the big local tournaments, therefore, I chose a NOGI competition (i.e. a 'no kimono' one, where you just wear shorts and a t-shirt), and then I looked at the list of competitors online.

I then sat back and breathed it all in. It was clear that I was entering a big, respected competition because the fighters were hailing from all across Britain. Called 'Kleos', up for grabs is not just a gold medal, but a gigantic, metal, Thor-style" hammer for the person who wins the Absolute category, which is where all the winners in their weight divisions come together to see who is the mightiest of them all.

But when I finally clicked online to sign up to the tournament, it was sold out. Phew, I thought, though I'm ashamed to admit it now. Maybe I won't have to compete after all.

And yet in the end, I do get a place: I'm to bring my £40 to enter the tournament with me when I arrive for my weigh-in. The question is: what weight will I be fighting at?

And this next bit really is a quandary. Will I diet a bit to bring my weight down so that I'm more powerful against smaller, lighter opponents, or will I not bother dieting, carry on eating the crisp sandwiches, and actually just fight someone who's very likely much taller and more built than me?

After all, at 87 kilos in weight on my bathroom scales, with a shapely pair of boobs, I was at that point just over the 'less-than-85-kilos' category.
I could make that weight, I reasoned. And yet, the category above was for fighters who weighed less than 91.5 kilos — which was basically a stone more than I weighed.

And then I thought: actually, no. The reason I'm doing this Jiu-Jitsu lark is because I'm basically scared of big, strong people.

So that's what I decided to do. I decided to fight in the heavy-weight division.

And yet, in the weeks leading up to the event, for all my braggadocio, in the gym I was still very nervous about rolling with big guys. I know Jiu-Jitsu is a martial art for the little man to swing and pin his far bigger opponent around on the floor, but that's providing you actually know how to do it. "It's like human chess," I'd hear people in the gym say. And I'd think, "Well, sure, to you guys it is. To me, it's like having Andre The Giant teabag you repeatedly in the face and there's nothing you can do about it."

I was still utterly terrified come sparring time. I didn't see me, a 40-year-old man, now, finally, at his lifetime physical fitness peak. Inside, I was still 7-year-old me, and delicate and malleable and scared.

In fact, I was still scared in exactly that same way I'd always been when things had gotten too out of hand for me. 'Delicate Me' wanted to cry big blobby tears like a child in a park who's gone down a slide fact-first with horrific consequences, and now can't find his mum. Grown-up 'Angry Me', meanwhile, wanted to use all my strength in a sudden act of aggression to defend myself (which is, ironically, a big no-no in sparring unless you want to completely burn yourself out in about 30 seconds flat).

The more balanced me though referred back to my secret mentor, Jocko. What is it he'd said to do when overcome by emotion? Ah yes: 'Normal Face'.

Basically, when life gets too on top, he'd say, don't get all depressed or scared or sad or angry. Just make your face completely expressionless, relax every muscle, and just do 'Normal Face'.

It sounds insane, doesn't it? Except it's not. It actually works. By not making any expression at all, your adrenaline and fears instantly dissipate, as if your face muscles control your emotions, and they're directly linked to them. Try it! Terrified? Do Normal Face. It actually works. (The divorce court's just here, take the first left).

And so that's what I started doing whenever my mind suggested to me that I should start panicking. IMMEDIATE NORMAL FACE. The fear would disappear. The day would move on. And I'd forget all about that emotion that I was about to get in a tizzy about.

That said, I did have to still think about how to fight big guys from a tactical standpoint, despite being as non-emotive about it as I could be.

With big guys, you see, they know they're big, so for them they can just put all their heft on you until your eyeballs pop out of your head like a Tom and Jerry cartoon. Big guys; they are all about pressure. And so, for the lighter fighter, you can't play their game. You have to roll around them and wiggle about.

Not that this ever worked in my experience as a white belt. For me against the big guys, the end result often just saw me having the life crushed out of me.

Which in its own way, isn't a bad thing because you're learning not to panic while someone the size of King Kong squashes all the air out of your lungs while crushing your rib cage.

And actually, in your mind, as the life is being crushed out of you, and all around you fades to dark as they subsume you in their heft, all you're really thinking is, "If I were on the edge of death, are the people in this room responsible enough to not let me die?"

But actually, against these mega-monsters, and with every other weight below, I did notice that the more you chill out, the more your breathing slows, and the more it's no longer that much of a biggie.

And the funny thing is, when people are crushing you to death, or even choking you to the point where you feel your head is going to pop off, frequently amongst us lower belts, the person choking you out tends to get bored.

If they can't submit you with a position in about 10 seconds, they just think, "Oh, bloody hell, it's not working."

And then they move onto another position.

At which point you can switch your hips to the side and create some space between you and the monster trying to crush you.

That was my reading of it, anyway. And let's be clear here: after more than a year, and then two years, and then more, of pretty intense commitment, training at least four times a week, I was still shockingly rubbish.

And yet, as one advanced Jiu-Jitsu player said to me after I asked him to critique my ability to see how I could improve, "You are where you should be. You're a white belt."

Which made me think just how long it takes to get good at this sport.

In other martial arts, from what I gather — such as Japanese Jiu-Jitsu, for example — it seems like you can get to black belt in about five years.

But BJJ requires an amount of time commitment that seems insane.

Honestly, the amount of hard work and exhaustion I put in over months and months and months of training and trying my best, I could have probably filled 25 buckets full from my face-sweat alone.

And what's more, I gave it my all, my everything, as Barry White used to say. And yet not only was I still mediocre, I also couldn't think how to flow the moves together so that they all linked in a sequence to incapacitate my sparring partner. A big guy would just flatten me, and I'd think, "Yup, I have absolutely nothing in my head right now — no techniques whatsoever to counter this, nothing!"

And that's what it was like month after month.

But I was on a journey, I reminded myself — a journey to overcome my fears.

And so, one Saturday morning, petrified to death, I packed my Jiu-Jitsu gi, gum shield, and ear guards, and drove up the motorway to my first Jiu-Jitsu tournament, praying that one of my car tyres might blow out before I got there.

CHAPTER ELEVEN

As the miles ticked by in the car, I told myself that whatever I did, I mustn't keep coming forward like I'd been advised to by my dad as a boy, and yet at the same time I forgave him for giving me such appalling advice when it came to fighting.

I was now on my own now. I would fend for myself. I was setting out to finally put myself up against not just the bullies who'd tormented me in my early teens, or the little bastards who'd relentlessly mugged me as a teenager.

No. I was now putting myself up against grown men who, even though they were white belts, fancied themselves in a fight; guys who, now like me despite our white belt limitations, reckoned that if push did one day come to shove, we'd have a little something in our arsenals in order to fight back.

This fight, no matter how badly I did, would represent the moment I finally broke free from all my hang-ups about being such a supreme wimp.

I was standing up to my fears.

I knew that I'd likely be terrible. I was still rubbish at fighting. Truth be told, I barely knew the rules of Jiu-Jitsu.

And if someone had explained them to me, I still probably wouldn't have been able to make heads nor tails of them.

So now here I was, with the opportunity to rescue the little boy who still lived in my head, whose framework for one's entire personality had been built as a defence mechanism out of the embers and ashes of every beating I'd ever received as a child.

As I ate the ham sandwiches I'd packed for the hour-long car journey to the event, I didn't think about what moves I'd use to attack or defend myself in my fight, due to take place in the next two hours. All I thought about was not eating so much chocolate that if someone leant on me too hard, what with all that slowly digesting ham in my stomach, I'd crap on the mats.

Truthfully, that's the kind of stuff you think about when you know you're fighting in public. Sometimes, even, in fact, when you roll with someone at your gym after eating a big dinner 40 minutes earlier.

You might have a fart in the chamber, for example. But what can you do other than hold it in and hope to goodness you don't let rip. Because it is distracting. You've got a guy crawling all over you, and you're supposed to defend yourself and just really all your bum hole lips are doing is pulling themselves in so you don't humiliate both yourself and your sparring partner.

One guy I once rolled with — this big, sweaty, hairy, heavy metaller-type who was actually very sweet-natured, did such a loud fart as he landed on his back that I had to ignore it completely. It was just too big a fart. So I had to go into NORMAL FACE plus deaf grandpa mode to save his honour. I mean, where do you go from there?

"Oops, I probably shouldn't have had that big meal before I came here," he'd said ruefully, embarrassed, while I demurred and said I thought it had been his foot slipping on the gym mat (while fitting a World War One-era mustard gas mask over my face).

Elsewhere, when someone farts on the mats accidentally, either the whole class looks up from sparring and laughs at the situation. Or everyone ignores it, knowing that they've got more pressing worries on their hands, like the bloke they're rolling with trying to smash past their defences.

Yet back in my car and hurtling up the motorway towards my first fight, admittedly I had more pressing, non-fart-related, thoughts flowing through my mind.

Weirdly, in fact, simply knowing that I'd decided to have a proper fight, with a stranger who was going to try to tear my head off, in itself felt like a huge personal win.

I knew that really the whole thing was down to chance and a bit of luck, maybe with a tiny smidgeon of learnt experience at this level as a white belt.

Despite my best efforts, and hours of training, you see, my ability to fight a live person steaming at me was very still unimpressive. I knew that.

So in many ways, just knowing that I'd had the balls to sign up for a nationally recognised tournament involving clubs from across Britain, all vying to smash each other to bits, was in itself the end of my journey.

I hadn't buckled. I hadn't cowered. I was doing something that would most likely terrify those very individuals who'd taken so much pleasure in bullying me as a child.

They were weak, I now realised. And I was... less weak.

It felt like a breakthrough for 7-year-old Me.

Ninety minutes later, I pull into the car park of the large judo competition hall where the event is being held. All different types of people from a multitude of backgrounds and of all ages are entering and exiting the event.

That's the thing with Jiu-Jitsu, I realise. It's almost impossible to tell who the killers are.

Yes, if they have wonky, stuck-out ears, thick necks and athletic physiques, that tends to be a giveaway.

But with this sport, it's not always that simple. Often a tiny little guy with perfect ears and a nerdy demeanour who's actually a solicitor or works in IT can, in truth, be the biggest beast on the mat you can imagine, twisting you and contorting you into all kinds of demented positions before choking you out. Which is what you hear military people who've been to war say; that it's often not the big steroid-y guys who display bravery and courage beyond the call of duty. In most cases, it's that shopkeeper from that small village; the most un-hotshot, non-physically impressive bloke you can imagine. Grit, it seems, is internal and technique comes from application over time, trying hard and keeping an open mind. Often, I realise, the massive guy who tries to intimidate you or barks wildly at you isn't necessarily the guy who'll finish you off.

And the guys who can finish you like that can also be of any age. It's not just the young guns in Jiu-Jitsu who know a thing or two. It's not like sports like boxing or football, where age is instantly and visibly detrimental during live matches. An older guy will make up for loss of strength — for the loss of springiness that comes with advancing years — by adapting his game.

That's why it's often mesmerising to watch an older guy applying all this technique to a fight with a young guy who's pure 'Hulk-smash'. In X-Men parlance, it's like watching Magneto playing mind-games with a young buck Colossus.

Like everything in society, it seems, youthful assertiveness is important, but only up to a certain level.

In the end, it's competence that wins.

When you hear guys in the gym refer to another guy as 'a beast' or 'a savage', what they really seem to be saying is: "That guy's level of competence — the speed at which his mind solves ever-changing physical riddles — is remarkable."

An 'Einstein' at Jiu-Jitsu in other words beats a massive, enraged nightclub doorman every day of the week.

Nevertheless, walking from my car towards the Jiu-Jitsu hall right now, I was overcome with a sense that this was it. It was on. It was real.

The question was whether I'd bitten off more than I could chew. Just how badly would I get humiliated in front of everyone watching?

I enter the building and follow the stairs up and round to a drinks bar and cafe, overlooking the large hall below, revealing two large mats where two batles are being fought simultaneously.

The weigh-in to my fight is due to take place within the next hour.

Ten minutes after that, I'm on.

But looking down at those bouts below, taking place behind that glass wall I'm peering through, I hesitate. I feel as if the entire structure of my sphincter is about to collapse through my legs, as if my intestines are only just hanging on inside me by a thread.

Down there, amidst the crowd, and the referees in their striped tops, and the judges sat behind overlooking tables, scoring the fights... down there is struggle, and sweat and aggression. Down there it's the unknown. Down there it's really happening: fighters are being put in positions against their wills to the point where they're on the verge of passing out.

Up here, by the bar, overlooking the fights, there's a lady putting hamburgers on a barbecue in time for lunch, and there's lager on tap.

That lady doing the hamburgers. She's so relaxed. The bar staff are relaxed. The whole vibe is 'sunglasses yellow face emoji'. Up here, it's a weekend afternoon, a lazy day of comforting roasts and a nap with the papers. Down there, though, it's pain and humiliation and fear and 'mind-blank' as you freeze up trying to remember the sequence of that special move of yours, while some massive bloke from Leicester who you've never met before, who probably ate his own mum's face for breakfast, tries to justify the financial cost of his trip on the basis of just how much he leaves you looking like a human soup. These people would shake my hand then steal my soul. And they all looked so strong and powerful down there. They were muscle and bone. I was loose skin and gravy. I was scared.

Plus I couldn't hear any sound from downstairs as it was blocked out by the glass, which added to the sense of foreboding. I was looking at was a few hundred people staring at fighters on the mat, while these monsters due to shortly fight each other limbered up on the side-lines. The vibe was basically like a Victorian pistol duel: good manners — and then murder.

I wasn't so sure I wanted any of this. Plus I felt genuinely scared that when I went downstairs to the fight-level, everyone would stop and stare at me and say, "What the hell are you doing here? You're shit."

I'd then freeze up, and accidentally trip over, a bit like Inspector Clouseau in The Pink Panther films, pulling the entire strip-lighting and roof down with me, thereby bringing the event to a close.

No, I told myself. Be tougher. Be stronger. Be someone else...

And yet, trying to harden up in the moment was easier said than done, in spite of how much this martial art had taught me about overcoming my fears. Jiu-Jitsu had so far shown me that when life — or an insanely wild opponent built like Optimus Prime — comes swinging at you, you don't buckle. You don't crap your pants. You don't freeze up and hesitate and mumble to yourself, 'Oh, God, I can't do this...'

Instead you stay as loose as a goose and just totally chill out. You relax your body language and look at the bad stuff coming at you full force, but with an air of detachment. That's the theory, anyway.

Freeze up, though, and it's basically your precursor to rigor mortis. Do that, I reminded myself, and you're going to get smashed.

Yet time for reflecting was now over. It was time to walk downstairs to the mats now. And I knew this. I'd just have to put on my big boy pants, as my wife likes to say, and face the music, whatever it may be.

And so, feeling my belly do 'The Worm' on my bladder, I gathered myself, tightly gripped the bannister at the top of the stairs and worked my way down towards the shouts and screams of enthusiasm emanating from the wide-open swing doors to the main event.

Through those open doors and into the hall I went. I caught the attention of some people but only in the most normal of ways: no one pointed me out to their friends or started laughing that it's me, mocking me, as, 'that lousy white belt'.

In fact, everyone in this hall just seemed very polite, focusing most of their attention on the battle their teammates were currently embroiled in on the mats.

And although the sounds of Led Zeppelin playing on the overhead speakers helped wrap me up into the energetic cut and thrust of the event, it also dawned on me that I owed it to myself to do my best. Having been beaten up by black, brown, purple, blue and multi-stripe white belts many, many times before at my home academy, and having still lived to tell the tale, truthfully, how bad could this possibly be? I decided to give it my all, to try and stay relaxed, and do the best I could do.

I was here now, I reasoned. And in life, as they say, just showing up is half the battle won.

I head to the changing room, sign in, get changed into my NOGI outfit — a t-shirt, shorts and my knee pads — then stand on the scales. I easily make weight because I'm so light for my division. I'm just over its threshold.

So, in essence, I'm giving up a lot of weight to those bigger men who may decide to starve themselves down to fight the smaller guys in the division below in order to gain a weight and power advantage. While I was barely making heavyweight, some of these other guys were potentially boiling themselves down from the ultra-heavy category. Still, best not to dwell on that, I decided. I'd just throw myself in there and do my thing.

After all, I came to this sport because I wanted to learn how to submit bigger men, to no longer be terrified and manhandled by giants.

I wanted to be the small guy capable of blasting the big bullies to bits, even though that was a prospect that might take me at least eight years of Jiu-Jitsu, up to purple belt, to achieve. Because what other better social confidence builder could there possibly be?

Now warming up and getting the blood flowing, I reasoned that this fight would be like every other roll I'd ever had in the gym. When, while sparring in the academy, had I not tried my very hardest? Every single roll I'd ever had involved me giving it my very all simply on the basis that I didn't want to get killed or squashed by my opponent.

So, I'd treat this fight in just the same manner, I told myself. It was 'just another roll'. Just another live body coming at me, a new terrifying set of limb- and weight-related problems to solve.

With that in mind, I reminded myself about some of the basics: 'Don't let him get past your legs and crush you,' I told myself. 'Don't stick your arms out so that he can bend them back against themselves. Stay in a ball, roll around, and try not to get hurt. Don't give him what he needs.'

I was now no longer the same person I had been when I'd started Jiu-Jitsu. And that alone felt like a personal victory. I felt insulated and protected by how far I'd come as a person.

I'd made myself proud.

I no longer needed to rely on what my Dad had fallaciously told me about continuing to 'keep coming forward no matter what'. I had my own version now on what would hold me in good stead (even if my own version was also fundamentally and technically flawed). I was happy to be here at this fight, and ultimately, I told myself, I'd be fine.

In the distance I could now hear my weight category being called to 'Mat 2'.

All of a sudden, it became very real.

I felt a surge of adrenaline pool in my stomach, making me feel sick.

Limbering up, and shaking out my legs, more to keep my anxiety at bay than to get my muscles loose, I was placed in a line-up facing the mat with four other guys. All of them were either bigger or stronger than me. One in particular looked very athletic.

He was tall and wiry with muscle. The other two looked ready to fight but didn't look as in the zone.

I tried not to make eye contact with any of them. I didn't want to connect with them in any way. I didn't want to let my guard down. I didn't want to break my focus.

Essentially, I was scared, I knew I was scared, and I knew that my opponents were here to win. I was also aware that by connecting with them on a human level I'd become too engaged and let all my defences down — and then be shocked when the fight started that they'd be trying to hurt me mercilessly when

I thought we were now friends, having just shared a common bond.

I tried to empty my mind of all memories of the multitude of times I'd been tapped out by my opponents over and over and over again often within a one five-minute round. Reminding myself of how beatable I was, how easily I tapped under the weight of someone stronger than me, was knocking my confidence.

As the minutes ticked by, moreover,I could feel my confidence slump, my shoulders rounding down, my head sinking, in many ways almost giving in to the idea that I was going to be smashed any minute now. I knew that I was puzzle that most opponents could solve over and over and over again from many different angles, using many different approaches.

Yes, I'd try my hardest, but deep down a voice was telling me that, really, I knew which way this would go.

But, that's how the mind works, or my mind at least, as daft as I sound. And I was hoping that their mind would therefore now be going totally insane with panic while I maintained a veneer it calm.

I peer up at my opponents to see if they're as scared as I am. Nope! These guys are here to party; to really go for the win.

I shake hands with my first opponent on the mat, then we both shake hands with our referee in the middle of a sports hall that suddenly feels as expansive as an open field with tiny me being looked down on from a helicopter.

IT WAS NOW ON.

"FIGHT!" says the ref.

And we're off so fast I don't have enough time to process my own panic.

My opponent comes at me, a short, stocky guy covered in tattoos, and he has no intention of making friends or warming into it.

We're in a standing position and, as is typical of me my entire life, I'm not the one who attacks first, which is a mistake.

"Be first," I've heard boxing coaches on the TV shout at their fighters.

And they're right: the attacker gets the psychological advantage because he's making the move and his opponent is instantly on the defence. And it's hard to quickly switch from defending yourself to counterattacking, at least at my level anyway.

So anyway, this guy is grabbing me and pulling me by the back of the neck and all I can think is, "Holy crap, what the hell is happening here?" And also, "Wowsers, I actually have no techniques in my head to take him down. I don't know any. What do I do? I'm knackered. I'm getting exhausted. How can I be so exhausted? I shouldn't have eaten that ham sandwich. I think I need a poo. Oh, God..."

We're now wrestling furiously, both of us using our strength, which is the antithesis of Jiu-Jitsu.

"BJJ is about technique, not physical strength," I remind myself. "So calm down!"

I jump up, wrap my legs around his waist and bring him down to the mat.

But he's not even recognising that move. He's going for my neck at 100 miles per hour.

He wants to flatten me, to crush me. "This isn't Jiu-Jitsu," I think in a blind panic. But it is: it's white belt Jiu-Jitsu.

This is a wild street fight, just without punches.

He needs to slow down.

Wow. I do really quite need him to slow down. I'm so busy trying to keep him off me, in fact — and so physically tense — that I'm almost completed gassed out.

Somehow I manage to roll to my side, and put my weight on him.

I'm covered in his sweat, and he's covered in mine. He's also begun accidentally dribbling a bit and sweating all over my face and into my mouth like an unintentional mad man. If I wasn't shitting my pants so badly, I might have had the headspace to mumble, "Er, I'm so sorry, but you appear to be emptying the contents of your mouth and entire guts into *my* mouth which is a little bit slightly dark side. Would you mind ever so much — "

But I don't.

Because my bum flaps are blowing like loose tarpaulin in a hurricane.

I try to pin him to the ground, but he now moves his hips out and tries to push me backwards. "Move the hips, twist the hips, it's all in the hips," I recall one of the coaches from my academy saying. And he's doing just that, making my life tough. It's like trying to cuddle a huge blob of jelly.

As heavy and as hardcore as he's being, however, my mind starts to clear and I begin to see reason. The shock of the fight dissipates. Yes, this is what they call a 'classic white belt death match', with effectively just two blokes wrestling without any skills, unable to finish each other, and exhausting ourselves in the process. But wow, are we going for it.

I need to start using my brain, I think. I need to let my body go where it needs to.

Luke Skywalker-style, I need to close my eyes and use the force, to feel where my body weight drifts to, as mind and body meld to become one, so that I can just flow around this marauding beast and control him. More Jedi Knight, I tell myself, and less 'Jar-Jar Binks on the brink of soiling himself.' In short, I need to lose control of my body and mind to gain control in this fight.

And roger me sideways with a rubber chicken, it's working. It's working!

It's bloody working! I am Neo. I am at one with The Matrix, I know Kung-Fu. Take that, Agent Smith, you shit, how d'ya like them — "

Slaggy McFuckbuttocks, I've been swept.

I'm back on my back again and this lunatic with my murder on his mind is not letting up.

However I can tell now that he's all power and no technique because he's gassed himself out so badly. For him, it's just kill or be killed. And although he was until this point doing the killing, now he looks like someone who needs a quiet weekend break at a spa. He's ruined himself.

Calming down despite the cries from my coach and fellow fighters about what I need to do ("Not that! Not that! Jesus, haven't you learnt anything, you fat, useless bastard?"), I feel my mind and heart slow down.

I imagine that I'm my coach. He's never tense when he rolls. For him, it's all about control and technique. His sense of calm and fun when rolling exudes confidence both outwards and inwards. So I think, sod it, ok, imagine you're him.

I imagine my man boobs that jangle up and down like comedy shop googly-eye glasses suddenly disappearing. My back broadens, which in real-life would just mean more back hair over a larger surface area.

My legs get large. I imagine myself as a powerhouse; a technical lump with explosive speed.

"The problem with white belt fights is that no one knows much technique — so in competitions it's just a vicious brawl," I recall one high-level teammate saying about white belt tournaments, reinforcing the idea that this is just a white belt death match after all.

"That's why I'm glad I'm not a white belt anymore. Those fights are just brutal."

And he's right, I think, as my opponent appears to rub his undercarriage up and down my face like my head is a cheese-grater, and his undercarriage perhaps a block of Parmesan cheese. At white belt we are all talentless and brutal because we're flailing around like men threatened by the prospect of a vicious castration should we — god forbid — lose a fight that actually stands for very little (unless you're the one fighting, in which case these fights feel like everything).

But the truth is: at white belt, we're generally so clueless that all we've got is our existential roar, plus 25% of the end part of a technique we think we know but have half-confused with some other confusing claptrap we've watched on YouTube.

And yet — and yet! These are the parameters that everyone in this competition has to operate within, I reason.

And as brutal and as much of a struggle as this match right

now is, the quicker I end it with technique, the less mindless it'll be.

Strength and power and aggression might be the order of the day for a white belt battle, but it's going to be technique, I tell myself, that finishes this fight.

That said, to the people watching this fight, or any white belt fight, who actually know how to wield Jiu-Jitsu's power, it must be like watching two X-Men children trying to unleash their superpowers on each other, but misfiring all over the shop because we haven't got a bloody clue how to harness it.

It's tragic. It's comedic. And yet, for us white belts in there, holy crap: it feels like it's life or death!

Continuing to imagine myself as a technical 800-pound beast without human empathy — like a Terminator robot covered in a human body (but perhaps with the body shape of Father Christmas), I squash my full mass down on my opponent, and he groans.

And this is the messed-up thing about Jiu-Jitsu: to hear your opponent groan (but not in actual pain because in the case I'm describing he's tired, and thankfully not actually injured) is, I'm ashamed to admit, a huge ego boost. That he's expressed discomfort is like an opposing poker player suddenly pulling an expression like Munch's 'The Scream.' You know at that point, for all your sins, that your opponent's armour, his pride, has taken a dent.

I don't feel good about saying this, but it's true. The moment your opponent groans… you're getting to him.

And with my opponent here, he's thoroughly exhausted himself after going so balls-to-the-wall in this fight for so long.

His gas supply is really, really dwindling now and he knows it.

His strategy of 'kill at speed' has been his undoing. As he turns into me, I pin him to the mat by putting all my weight through my knee on his belly.

He groans and turns into me. And that's when I see it: he's about to give me the chance to guillotine him.

Shiiiiiiiiiiiiit! This might work. All the sound around me drops off. Will I get it? Will I get it? Is he setting me up, knowing that I'm going for it, with the intention to sweep me in some way and put my back on the mat.

Who cares, I think. I'm going to go for it.

I push my knee down hard again onto his stomach then reach my left arm around his neck.

Now connecting my hands, I rotate my right elbow up, closing the space between the circle I've created with my hands and his throat. I also make sure that the sharp bit of my wrist is cutting into his Adam's apple. (Hey, chill — that's the game).

It comes on quickly and he starts to splutter, but I want this over quickly and so thrust my hips into his chest, cranking his neck even more, even though it should feel like a cutting motion on my opponent's neck — and not a crank. It's only a matter of time, surely. He's got to tap. This must be excruciating.

I feel a gentle tap-tap-tap on the side of my left thigh, like the world's tenderest Mini-Me hand saying to my leg, "Enough."

It's a submission from him in both his body and his mind. I beat him. I outthought him, he's saying with that tap, and there's nowhere left for him to go. The better man (although only marginally), in this instance, has won. But good lord, that was hard work!

I instantly let go in that horrified way that most people who roll do in the knowledge that most people wait far too long to tap and you just hope the opponent underneath you suffering temporarily at your hands is actually okay.

It's a sport, after all. Technique versus technique. Nothing personal. Just (in my case, bad) Jiu-Jitsu.

We both stand up and embrace. He has humility in his eyes, mixed with gratitude, and I have nothing but thanks to offer him along with ginormous hugs. In the eyes of our judge, one of the greatest black belts competing in the UK at this time, what he just witnessed was effectively the equivalent of a 5-year-old child trying to make a roast. Just a freaking disaster of technique, blubber, sweat and nonsense. I mean, honestly, what in THE HELL had I just put in front of his eyes. Nevertheless, I'd won.

And as the ref grabs mine and my opponent's wrists, then turns us to face the audience to raise my hand, I feel absolutely elated.

However, I'm under no illusion that I'm now the next great thing to happen to the sport. It's like your toddler showing you a single massive blob of paint on a scrap of A4 and looking up at you, waiting for your mouth to be agape like you'd just looked into that shining briefcase in Pulp Fiction. I mean, honestly. It was just dreadful Jiu-Jitsu.

Yet all I could think was: 1) I love this opponent for having brought out the best in me; 2) This is wonderful, magical, this is the real me — and I won!; and 3) Oh, my bloody God, I'm knackered. Completely knackered.

The moment he'd tapped and I'd stood up, moreover, I'd raised my hand to the air as if I was in a classroom. And I've confused myself by doing that.

I don't really knock why I did that in fact. It wasn't to show off. It was more like I was raising my arm to be pulled out of that tide of sweat and exhaustion and hard work I'd just been drowning in. As if to say, "Ok, world. You can pull me up back to safety now, thanks!"

Either way, I'd won. And as the air came back into my lungs, and the sweaty fog of confusion cleared from my eyesight and mind, the concept that I'd been victorious began to corkscrew its way through my brain. I'd…won.

Which meant it was now me and the winner of the previous fight to see who'd get the gold medal and the first place podium finish.

So that meant I was, yes, going to win a silver medal, which was awesome, but it also meant that for my next fight, I'd have to grapple with that tall, athletic, powerful bloke. He was bigger than me, stronger than me, and if I saw him in the street and he started on me I'd think, 'Hmm, crikey, he's a bit of a lump,' and I'd panic.

So, with the prospect of fighting him now on the horizon

within the next ten or so minutes, I did what all action heroes might do: I stuck my head in the sand and tried to ignore the fact that I'd be facing someone even tougher than the last guy.

I did this by striking up a conversation about family life with a friend from the gym. He'd just moved towns with his wife and children, so we had a good old chat about the benefits of moving to the countryside where life is slower and possibly happier.

But really, what I was doing here was going on the psychological defensive. I was taking my mind out of the fight because I was scared. Terrified. I wasn't thinking about fighting positions I'd feel confident in in the face of my forthcoming fight. I wasn't saying to myself, 'Right, I'll lock my legs around him, push one of his arms in, keep his other arm out, then triangle choke him.'

Instead, what I was doing was civilising myself in a conversation that made all my focus and aggression and will to win dissipate.

"Sorry, I should stop talking so that you can concentrate on your fight," my friend then politely points out.

"No, it's cool," I say, just masking the fact that what I'm really saying is, 'Please don't go, don't leave me. You're normal and kind and I know you, but out there it's a bear pit.'

"If I lose my next fight, that's fine," I lie. "For me, the victory is just taking part. I've overcome my fear anyway — fighting big people — just by showing up."

Which is the biggest load of codswallop you can ever imagine. I wanted to win. But he was big and I was scared.

What I'd really meant to say to my friend was, "Look, I'm going to lose the next fight because he's big and I'm scared. So I might as well just drop all veneer of hardness and aggression and give him the fight. He's big, I'm small. He's hard. I'm small, bald with big hairy jangly comedy tits. I'll quit now while the going is good."

Which is the most harmful self-talk you can ever summon.

Let me be clear: you need to go in there and think at all times, "Within the confines of the rules and my skills, I am going to make this guy's life miserable until he taps. It's not a tickling competition. I need to harden up or he's going to go in there and break my heart — and then take my heart."

You need to be the aggressor, I've since learnt, even when you appear to be in a less-than-dominant position.

But because my mentality in the gym had always been 'just defend and survive', I'd hardwired myself to respond to danger by effectively running scared. That is not how you do it.

You do it by intellectually outmanoeuvring your opponent, smashing past his defences then making him tap. You don't use strength. You don't tighten up. You flow. You move. You enjoy yourself. But what you don't do is say, "Well, it's a hurricane. What can I do?"

No — you attack! But I was drained by fear.

And now here I was, soon back on the mats for the final. For the gold medal. And I'm having a wobble. I've seen this guy's Jiu-Jitsu. Technically, we're where we should be for white belts. He isn't great. Neither am I. So what have I got to lose?

Yet the fear of the unknown makes me freeze up.

He shakes my hand and I look up at him. Right, I tell myself. Strengthen your body and senses for impact. He's going to come at you, like the last bloke. But harder. He wants this gold. Do you?

"Yes," I was saying in my head. But was it even possible?

Again, this is exactly how you don't go into any altercation, in any capacity, in any sphere in life.

We slap and bump hands, the customary 'let's dance' fighter's handshake before battle in Jiu-Jitsu. It's a polite way of saying, 'Right, let's do this! You ready? Cool. Me too.'

And bang! Lanky Goliath grabs me around the back of my neck and with the other hand he tries to throw me off balance. And the funny thing is, in Jiu-Jitsu, running away from the fight is the opposite of what you need to do, though every fibre in your being wants to. You need to run towards the war, not away from it.

The closer you get to your opponent, it turns out, the less space you create for him to manoeuvre you; and the closer you are to him in order to start bullying him.

However, because I can't remember any takedown moves, and I've just got this monster grabbing hold of me, all I can think is: just wrap both legs around him and bring him to the floor. Then I'd have him locked within my control, with my legs clamped around his waist.

I do that and we both tumble to the ground, with him on top of me and me on my back.

But the problem with me being on my back and him trying to push my legs away from his waist so that he can clamber on top of me is that I don't really have any moves to do from here.

There are moves I sort of know. But I've never successfully pulled them off in sparring with my teammates, so what makes me think I can pull them off now.

What do I do?

Well, I just beat the last guy with a guillotine choke, I reason. So maybe I'll try that again.

So I let him out from my legs, and backside my arse up, and wrap my left arm round his neck. He ducks down and my arm fails to catch around his neck. Which makes sense. How can I hope to submit someone when I'm not even in the right physical position to finish them? It won't work.

But I try again anyway, and again, and again, and again. And every single time he sees it coming and moves his head away from me.

'Stop doing the same bloody thing,' I tell myself.

'WELL, WHAT ELSE AM I GOING TO DO?' I shout back at my brain. 'I HAVEN'T GOT ANY OTHER THOUGHTS IN MY HEAD — YOU IDIOT!'

And so, I pop up to my knees and try to push him back. He responds by wrapping his legs around me. And now I'm trapped.

I try to push his legs down to the mat to get out of his 'closed guard' — his legs are completely wrapped around my waist — but it's no good. I can't escape. I'm bolted to the ground by the heaviness of his thighs.

Nevertheless, I give it one last go to pop up into a standing position. And although I sort of manage it, he sticks his right arm under my left leg so that I tumble backwards.

He then charges towards me and we wrestle some more. And then I'm back in his closed guard, again!

And I'm sweating like a bastard now. I'm really blowing hard, exhausted. And he knows it. He knows that's he's better than me at Jiu-Jitsu. He also seems happy about the fact that he's stronger and taller than me.

I look up from sweating involuntarily in floods all over his face, and notice on the judges' scoreboard facing the mat that he's seven points ahead of me (I've scored zero points to his seven).

And I'm panting and groaning in pain like a man giving birth to a dinosaur out of his rectum. But in BJJ, it's very hard to hide the truth, mainly because you're so close to your opponent — sometimes a matter of millimetres — and you can feel their strength and capabilities or lack thereof almost immediately while wrestling them.

So this guy knew he had me completely. And I knew it too.

However, saying to your opponent mid-competition," Ooh, I love this song!" as the AC/DC rock track, Back In Black, comes on through the event's overhead speakers, as he then did to me, is surely the ultimate liberty.

He clearly had such a lack of respect for my ability that he felt he could psychologically disengage from our fight.

Which in hindsight is hilarious.

But in the heat of the moment it blew my mind. "Ah, man. This is such a tune!" He starts singing the lyrics at me, half-closing his eyes in the moment, lost in the song's iconic lead guitar riff while I'm struggling to wiggle out from his control. And although I'm supposed to be in the middle of a fight with him, with me getting badly beaten up, and sweating everywhere through sheer exhaustion, I start laughing.

And although I continue to struggle desperately to get out from his guard, in the end it's just no good.

The ref calls time on the fight, but I am so psychologically locked into the fight, and by now so completely exhausted, that when he lets go of me, I immediately scramble back to his left leg and grab it to put a leg lock on him.

And then it dawns on me: nope, it's over.

I've lost.

We both stand up, the ref grabs our wrists and raises my opponent's hand in front of the crowd. I was happy I'd get the silver but I was still upset I'd lost.

And yet the truth was, he'd been so much better than me even though he was just a white belt.

My feelings about having won just by showing up are now completely dissipated and replaced by the fact that I could have had the gold. If only I'd been less rubbish.

I stand on the second-place step on the podium and receive my medal. Which felt great. I'd never won anything, at anything — ever, I think. Certainly nothing athletic. It was a big leap to go from being a terrified little fat boy getting beaten up in my best friend's bedroom to coming second in a national Jiu-Jitsu tournament.

But still, I was horrified by how empty of ideas I'd been during my fights. The first guy had come at me like a bull in a china shop, and the second guy had completely incapacitated me but not tapped me because like most white belts, he appeared to struggle to remember how to finish me.

I was filled with pride, but still my loss in the final reinforced in my mind that I was lacking.

My teammates were happy for me, too. They said, "Well done," and they were proud.

But as I stared at my medal in the car before setting off home, it dawned on me how far I'd still have to go — how much I'd have to progress — in order to one day win gold.

I also reflected on the fact that because I was 40 years old by this point, this meant all the guys in my category had to be over 35.

And so I told myself that perhaps a victory doesn't count in the old men divisions. Maybe if I was really brave I'd continue on my path to go up in weight — using weightlifting to get as heavy as I could go — as penance for my age. It was food for thought.

Nevertheless, I'd survived my first BJJ tournament. And I'd even gotten a medal. Silver wasn't gold, but it felt good.

I celebrated on the way home by pulling over at a service station and having a cheeky Nando's.

Sat in a booth, wolfing down chicken, felt completely knackered, as if my bones were all broken but thankfully encased in my skin so they didn't spill out in shards all over the floor.

I admit: it felt good to be a runner-up in a category at an event where everyone was trying their very hardest to beat the living hell out of each other, and I'd come second. I could live with second, for now.

CHAPTER TWELVE

When I phoned home to tell my wife and two daughters about my success at my first Jiu-Jitsu tournament, they were genuinely ecstatic for me.

That felt good. I'd sweated buckets in training over the past year-and-a-half. And — of course — the hard work had paid off. It was the oldest, truest maxim in the book. And yet here it was proving itself true again, certainly to me.

And that became the key takeaway for me. Hard work — unbroken hard work — is the answer. The key is to keep doing the thing you want to excel at day after day after day even though you may not feel like it. Just do it anyway. That's the lesson. The more you do it, the better you get. As long as you're maintaining pressure on the problem, eventually the problem changes shape and the issues you had before disappear. In the timeless words of Mike Tyson, "Discipline is doing something you don't want to do every day like you love it." And so that became my mantra.

Also, determined to never let myself feel that level of fear again in a tournament, I decided to double-down. From now on, starting the day after the tournament, I decided to train every single day, be it first thing in the morning or the last thing at night. And from that moment on, my ability and understanding really did start to improve.

I realised that actually going into a competition to just see what happens is futile. How can you hope for the best when you don't have an aim? You need to be constantly setting people up so that they fall into your traps. Not just going there to these competitions and hoping you don't die.

So then I really looked at what my strategy could be. Someone a bit better than me at Jiu-Jitsu, another white belt, told me that his whole game was working his way to his opponent's back in order to take the Rear Naked Choke, which is effectively a headlock from behind your opponent's head. I also saw him do it in competition. His whole aim was to take the guy's back. And he pulled it off.

I then attended a class a week later held by my instructor where he said to everyone: "You should always be looking to either take the mount [end up sitting on your opponent's chest] or take the back [with your arms and legs wrapped around their back like they're giving you a piggyback]."

And that was highly instructive. By having a direct strategy — going for the mount, for example — you're always on the offensive.

And by always being on the attack, it forces your opponent to take his mind off the traps he's setting for you, and instead focus on defending your attacks.

So from that point on, even if people weren't tapping to my attacks because I lacked the finesse to finish them, they were at least beginning to feel my pressure. Well, sort of.

I then asked a high-level blue belt I'd just sparred with what his game tended to be, and he said, "It depends on the person. But you're quite aggressive, so if I'm sparring you, I'll also try to be aggressive back."

Which shocked me because I was always the guy in Jiu-Jitsu waiting to be smashed by his opponent. And yet, just the mental note to start looking to take the mount or the back at all times completely upped my game (in that it actually gave me one). At least having an objective now forced me into a style of fighting that was giving my sparring partners at least a bit of a better run for their money. In short, where before I would get tapped in 30 seconds, now I might last up to a minute. It was still pathetic on my part, but it was statistically a 100% improvement on my part.

Whereas before, I'd been wild, now at least I was thinking about leverage and balance, and how to use my opponent's limbs as levers. I had a goal.

What's more, I examined my performance at my first tournament and thought, "Right, I don't know how to properly break someone's guard [remove their crossed ankles from around my waist], and I have zero takedowns."

So I saved a few videos from YouTube, most of them detailing how to escape these kinds of positions. And I watched them repeatedly.

Although knowing how to finish someone is key in Jiu-Jitsu, I needed to be realistic and accept that most of the time as a white belt I was in terrible positions I needed to get out of during sparring. Mastering escapes therefore, while also thinking about attacking constantly, became a priority.

Similarly, I discovered that many escapes end up with you in a more aggressive, attacking position, such as stuffing one of my opponent's legs between my own legs and then locking it off tight so they couldn't retrieve it.

This was a game-changer for me because it meant that I could, say, have King Kong on top of me, but as long as I had his leg stuffed between two of mine, I could rotate him around, and move him to and fro, often to my opponent's frustration.

Using that move really did change things for me because it meant I retained some control of my opponent, unlike usual.

And amazingly, my newfound approach to my flaws lead to a further wonderful development.

One evening at the end of a class, I was awarded two more stripes on my white belt.

Which felt amazing, even if it did instantly open up a new can of worms in my mind. Had my instructor made a mistake? He'd given me not one but two stripes, so I was now a four-stripe white belt.

Which means absolutely nothing in the world of Jiu-Jitsu. But in my little white belt world, it was perhaps one of the greatest moments of my life.

As my instructor shook my hand, said well done, and put two stripes around my belt, I stood there in disbelief.

I went back to stand against the wall where all my other classmates were lined up, and I didn't dare look down at my belt in front of everyone else.

I was just so shocked, but also so excited, that all I wanted to do was hold those four stripes up closer to my eyes. I felt giddy with pride and excitement. It was just two three-inch strips of white tape. But it was what each of those stripes represented, what I'd had to do to get them, all that effort I'd had to put in to earn them, that made me feel so fulfilled.

Yet I was still riven with uncertainty. One of my previous, and only, two stripes had come off my white belt through wear-and-tear a few months earlier and I hadn't replaced it. I had yet to hear my instructor announce to the class that we really must replace any stripes if they come unstuck. "They aren't magical amulets that only your instructor can replace," he joked. "If they come off, just put some fresh tape back on."

Yet as a white belt, you don't feel it's your right to stick your own ones on. It's daft, but there's a sense of the sacred about getting stripes, and so it doesn't feel acceptable to just bung your own stripes on. At the same time, you want to act like it's no big deal that a stripe fell off your belt, when of course, privately, it is.

Nevertheless, I now had unanswered questions about my own validity to be a four-stripe white belt. So I approached my instructor.

"Are you sure it was meant to be two stripes," I asked nervously. "One had fallen off, you see, so maybe you saw my belt, thought I was only a one-stripe white belt, and only meant to give me one more to make me a three-stripe white belt instead."

"No, it's meant to be four stripes," he replied. "How long have you been training, nearly two years?"

"Yes," I said, my toes curling in excitement.

"That's right. So it's four stripes."

Blown away, I thanked him — and then I realised later that actually four stripes on your belt in two years or thereabouts is pretty slow-moving.

Nevertheless, the next time I went training, that's when the real fear set in. I felt like an impostor, that I didn't deserve my four stripes. Three stripes, ok. But four stripes? How would I handle getting tapped by other white belts with fewer stripes? How would that make me look? How would that make me feel about my own ability?

And this is something I'd heard blue belts discuss in the gym changing rooms before with a smile on their faces. Their concern was that when they got promoted from white belt to blue belt, they suddenly felt hunted by white belts. And so they'd feel a pressure that if they then tapped to a white belt, their sense of self-worth would take a dint.

And that was a feeling that I could sense was now coming over me: a new need not to get tapped by someone with less than four stripes.

As one insightful new blue belt told me when I congratulated him for getting promoted, his rule being equally applicable to me now: "It's not quite the celebration that you think it's going to be. You spend almost two years looking up at blue belts above you, who've just tapped you non-stop, and then you're suddenly promoted. And rather than thinking, "This is the best day of my year," you think, "New stripe, or new belt, but same problems.""

And I agreed with his way of thinking. As happy as I was to receive those stripes, I also thought: "Yes, but I still have no measured, technical ability. I still flail around like a fish that's been caught at the end of a fishing rod."

When you're sparring higher belts, it always struck me as quite amazing how measured they were in pinning your limbs down so that they're putting unbearable pressure on your joints as they're slowly working their way past your defending legs and towards your chest, while your back's on the floor. In contrast to myself, every movement seemed to be thought through meticulously in many cases. They seemed to just be working through the move. Me, on the other hand? I was a sweaty disaster. And I think that's what the new blue belt had been alluding to. You may have received a wonderful honour in getting your new grading, but when an opponent is sat on your chest, for example, you're still the same person as you were yesterday, thinking, "God, now what do I do?" And to make matters worse, they say that you need to be good enough to defend whatever belt you are. So there's that added pressure too.

Which may explain the phenomenon I soon heard about, called 'blue belt-itis', which is when white belts who've spent two years trying to get to blue belt finally get there and either stop training as intensely — or stop training completely. Why? Maybe it's because in other martial arts they'd probably be a very high belt at this point, after putting in so many hours on the mats. So they think, relative to other martial arts, that they're pretty advanced fighters now. Perhaps it's because they've held the idea of getting a blue belt in such wonder for so long — they've held it up as such an awe-inspiring ambition — that when they finally get it, they've achieved their huge goal. They've run their marathon, so to speak.

And that's fair enough, I suppose. You can complete an entire university degree within three years, putting in roughly the same amount of hours as you do just to get a blue belt. And at university, that feels like an inordinate amount of time. It feels like a life section — a huge landmark of development for an individual. So when you get your degree you think, "Great, well that's for life now!"

But with a blue belt, there are still another three more belts to go including black belt, at which point they say that's when the real learning begins. And at blue belt alone, that means you've still got around another eight years left to get to black belt alone.

So when you get to blue belt, I imagined, and you still saw a ginormous marathon ahead of you, perhaps one would think, "Oh, bloody hell. I'm just a hamster on a wheel. When will it end?"

Perhaps, and this is more likely, new blue belts who gave up didn't quit immediately, I reflected. Yet having achieved this momentous landmark for a white belt, they thought, "Well, that's one huge chapter over with. I'll take a week off to rest. I deserve a rest."

Which they may do. But then that week off might become a month. Which becomes two months. And then maybe that's why blue belts are said to disappear.

Which was something I also wanted to do only two sessions later when, in spite of my new stripes, I was then tapped out by a ferocious white belt with no stripes whatsoever, which immediately snapped me out of my four-stripe mind-set.

I realised again that the real establisher of whether I was getting any better, whether in fact I would be able to handle bigger guys in a fight — on the mats or in the street — was whether I'd be able to cope with the heft of a big guy during a competition when they're going hell for leather, as that big guy did in my first fight.

And so I looked up at the board at my gym detailing the upcoming fights and put myself down for another competition.

Unlike my first tournament, this was a Gi-only competition, which meant I'd be now fighting in my kimono. So unlike NOGI, where both fighters are slipping around in each other's sweat, with limbs slipping out of each other's hands, the addition of the GI now meant we'd be able to grip each other and have something to grab, which meant we'd now have new opportunities for different kinds of chokes and locks, most of which still nevertheless eluded me.

It would definitely be a new competition experience, even if the prospect of entering into another bout was nerve-wracking.

That said, the addition of a new upcoming competition in my life added a ticking time bomb element to my training. I didn't want to feel that out of depth again in a competition, and yet I only had a short period of time to correct the numerous errors in the way I fought. Namely, I didn't really have any sweeps to dominate opponents with, and when I was on the top fighting, I was rubbish at using my body to put pressure on them to make them as uncomfortable as possible. You pressurise people so that they eventually make a move that exposes their weakest points, such as turning away from you. And in doing so, they give you the opportunity to catch them with a submission. The problem was, I was still having real problems even finishing my opponents.

I was also scared that I wouldn't do as well in my second competition as I had in my first, even though actually I was fairly terrible in my first.

I was haunted by that silver medal from my first competition. There it was hanging from a picture frame that had already been mounted there in the kitchen years earlier. My wife had proudly hung the medal around the sides of the frame like the frame was a person. And so every morning when I had breakfast, I'd look up from the table and see it. It just hung there, a sign that I'd actually achieved something and yet had still fallen short. I wanted gold now, badly, but would I even get bronze at my second competition? The fear of the unknown overcame me again.

CHAPTER THIRTEEN

Of course, I knew that at my level these fights meant nothing: at my first fight, I'd watched the judges watching the fighters who were white belts as they tangled with each other. And the expression on the faces of these judges was mild bemusement. They didn't mean to be rude or belittling. But in their eyes, their minds seemed to be saying, "I'm sorry, I just don't understand. How can these guys be so bad? How? How is it possible for someone to be so bad at Jiu-Jitsu? Is this even possible?"

It was like someone had transported them to a mystical world full of appalling, half-arsed takedowns and useless people just rolling around on each other like they were bundling a teammate who'd just scored a goal.

Their minds couldn't compute the insane shitness of our Jiu-Jitsu but yet they kept their sense of decorum and respect. They somehow held it together. Like you might at a children's school play, when all you really want to do is shout, "This is AWFUL!"

So sure. I knew that worrying about how my second Jiu-Jitsu tournament played out was about as ridiculous as trying to understand the rules of the WWE's Royal Rumble. "Who's winning?" "Who cares?"

But it meant something to me. Because I'd invested all my time in it. I'd thought endlessly about Jiu-Jitsu for the past two years. And whereas my first fight felt like a victory simply for the fact that I had turned up and didn't diarrhoea on the mats out of sheer terror during both fights, this second tournament had more riding on it. Why? Because if I failed to perform in this fight then it meant that the first tournament where I had won silver had been a fluke, and I really was a fraud. Not to others, but to myself.

My fear became a ticking time-bomb. As the month of my next tournament rolled around, I began to feel stiffer and stiffer in my legs.

Which was really the complete opposite of why I'd taken up this sport. My goal had been to learn how to deal with the prospect of having an unforeseen fight with a potentially far more powerful individual. And yet here I was getting stage fright leading up to a fight I'd been forewarned about. So really, if Jiu-Jitsu was there to stop me in my general life from having a wobble, then how come I was having a wobble? Granted, the opponent would be better most likely than the average man on the street. But now my fear had just changed shape and become relative.

What I really needed to do, therefore, was to just keep trying to roll with the biggest, hardest, scariest, angriest monsters in my gym. If, during sparring therefore, I was given the option to choose my opponent, instead of picking guys at my crappy level or just slightly worse so I could experiment with techniques, now I decided the best thing to do would be to get crushed by killers.

Whereas before I'd been trying to spar big guys to beat the fear out of me, now I was going for big guys who were also of much higher belts. I would scared the life out it myself so that I was no longer scared.

My thinking was that in the misery of getting repeatedly destroyed by killers on the mat, I'd become more battle-hardened. Yes, I'd have extremely limited success while sparring them. In fact, I'd get completely obliterated and tossed around and have panic attacks under their sheer squashing weight. But as long as I was trying my hardest, I would benefit by just surviving. I'd feel all that pressure and discomfort. I'd feel claustrophobic and suffocated under their mass. My limbs would be prized from my body and pulled into various locks and cranks. But if I gave it my all, then when I was with white belts in competitions, I wouldn't be as scared. I'd have something far worse to compare it to. And so I'd hopefully just calm down and focus on my plan of attack. With my utter fear of fighting removed, I'd actually be able to think through the fog.

And so, because it's considered bad manners to call out a black belt to spar you if you're any belt below them, I'd instead ask everyone up to and including brown belts with four stripes — the maximum number of stripes you can get before getting your next belt up — if they wanted to roll.

And understandably, their expressions were a mixture of confusion and bemusement. 'What the hell was I trying to say,' you could see them thinking? It's like asking Usain Bolt to sprint against you when you don't even know how to tie your shoelaces. And in the eyes of the advanced guys, they're thinking: "But we both know that I'll completely smash you. So why are we doing this?"

And they're absolutely right to think this. It's like a professor of maths competing against an 8-year-old with no real maths experience to see who'll win a maths test. It's a foregone conclusion who's going to win. When a white belt spars someone more advanced, getting submitted is not a case of 'if', but 'how soon'.

Nevertheless it felt vital to be able to roll with the highest belts, because the longer I survived, especially with the heavy guys, the more it would prepare me for the sudden onrush of aggression from fellow white belts in my next competition.

That a black belt as well as a brown belt I rolled with also said I'd definitely improved since the last time I'd sparred them was a massive bonus, even if what they meant was that I was definitely crap, but slightly less so. It lifted my self-belief. But more importantly, it blew me away how little they dwelled on the fact that they hadn't tapped me sooner. If I had been them and I hadn't tapped a white belt immediately I'd be confused about my own ability.

But the truth is, these guys weren't really trying: they were using me as a live dummy to practice their own game on without me even realising. Does a dad playing football with his young son even think about what he's doing as he farts around in the park? Absolutely not. He's just having some fun.

Meanwhile, my constant BJJ obsession was having other effects on my character. Jiu-Jitsu is so unique that it really

can steal your character. As you're talking to physically impos-
ing work colleagues who might be talking passionately to you
about their current frustrations, all you're thinking is, "Hmm,
interesting. However, if I wound my way around your body,
keeping my feet locked around your waist, I could then slip my
right arm around the front of your neck, then slip the top of my
left hand along the back of your neck for the Rear-Naked Choke.
And you would be completely and utterly defenceless."

Of course you don't really want to hurt or even touch a work
colleague, but it's symptomatic of how BJJ infiltrates the mind.
Every man you meet is squared up to work out how you would
deal with an opponent of that size. "Hmm," you're thinking,
"yes, he's big. And he could crush me with his weight. But if I just
got an under-hook on him from that position, I could sweep him
and take the mount..."

So that's what happens. New neural pathways corkscrew their
way into your mind so that a private thought about whether
Twix bars are overrated — they're not: you're thinking of Flakes
— will quickly divert into a fantasy drill where you're trying to
escape a very strong knee-on-belly from an opponent.

Which is why, when you tap out — very rarely, if ever —
a higher belt, there's an element of embarrassment from both
parties. You're both thinking, "We both can't stop thinking
about this bloody sport, so how the hell did a white belt just
win that roll?"

That said, the moment you tap a higher belt, you better pray
you have medical insurance. Because very, very rarely can a
higher belt not defend that belt he's wearing around his waist.
In most cases, in fact, you better bloody believe he's earned
every single moment of that ascension to a higher belt. Which
means if you tap him or her, they were probably just moment-
arily away with the fairies. And by God, are they now going to
drop the hammer on you.

But through all the sessions of me getting absolutely battered, I did have one epiphany: I realised that as long as your
technique is flawless (though easier said than done), very often

you can sweep a big guy just like you can sweep a smaller guy. You just have to find the right moment to take advantage of them being off-balance.

Still, as I continued to lift weights and get bigger so that ultimately I'd be able to handle myself when confronted by the biggest opponents on the mat, I exposed myself to a whole new problem.

With only a week to go before my second tournament — this time in the gi — I weighed myself. I was now only a fraction of a pound under the cut-off weight for someone fighting in the medium heavyweight bracket. And after looking at the weight categories that competitors would be fighting under, it turned out that no one was fighting in the direct weight category above. It was either fight at 88.3 kilos — an impossibility given that I was now 88.2 kilos (194 pounds) and the gi weighs up to 2 kilos. Or instead fight at the division above heavyweight, Ultra Heavy, which is for people who weigh more than 100.5 kilos (221 pounds).

So it was a case of diet all week to squeeze back into the medium heavyweight category. Or ask the organisers to put me in a category where the average guy I'd be fighting weighed 12.3 kilos (27 pounds) more than me, which is a lot of weight to give up.

Yes, I knew some Jiu-Jitsu by now, but with such a great weight disparity, it would have to be a case of me using only technique — or whatever technique I had. With big guys, you see, as a white belt, if you don't calm down when you're fighting them, you exhaust all your energy panicking just trying to get them off you before they flop themselves on top of you like a king-sized mattress. And then just submit you due to the pressure of their sheer weight alone.

And although I'd begun to have some success against bigger guys, mainly because I was now attacking constantly in order to stop them from having time to think, much of my success, I felt, came down to the fact that I was now a bit chunkier. I was eating loads and lifting loads. And I was growing accustomed to big guys just lying on top of my face and crushing my facial features back in on themselves.

I was also learning to cut off my emotions when these heffalumps were lying on me, so that I didn't constantly hyperventilate like I used to, and exhaust myself trying to push them off me.

But the heavier I got, and the less rag-doll-like my body became, the more I started seeing big guys for what they were. They were just human after all.

When you had them in bad positions on their back, often a position they're unused to given that they're usually overpowering others, they seemed to lose their shit more than the little guy who's been there a million times before and you just know has a terrible treat in store for you the very moment you shift your balance on him.

Some big guys are great at attacking, granted — but as with life, people who are used to bullying others sometimes don't know what to do when it's fired back at them. And although I was still only a white belt, I would occasionally see the frustration and confusion and hear it in the laborious breathing of big guys on the rare occasions I had them on their backs.

But that's not a given, of course. Most of the time with a bigger guy, they're crushing and smashing through you, especially if, worst case scenario, they're big and technical. So it's still very tough.

But as long as you can keep attacking them, and being a nuisance, I told myself, like those airplanes attacking King Kong, you may be lucky enough to find an opening.

So while my heart said: "Hmm, maybe I should not go to this competition after all, I'll just get smashed to bits by massive monsters," my head was speaking the truth to me. "You got into this sport in order to defend yourself against the biggest, most competent monsters out there. You're terrified of big people so go out there and fight the giants. Inoculate yourself to them!"

So that's what I decided to do: to keep trying to get bigger and keep trying to fight big men.

There was just one problem to this plan: six days before I was due to compete, while sparring a higher grade who kept tapping me out over and over and over again using triangle chokes and arm bars, my right ear started to swell up.

I ignored it and kept sparring. When you're charged up with adrenaline and covered in sweat, all you tend to care about is the fight, and trying to work out a way to tap him instead.

But my right ear was really taking a pounding. It was getting repeatedly knocked and bruised. By the time the session had ended and I'd returned to the dressing room after a shower, I looked in the mirror and took the image in. The top of my right ear was bubbling out. I had a cauliflower ear. Not just a bit of swelling and blackening like the first time. It was completely pumped-up. Squishy, like a small orb, full of custard.

I had to rush off to a work meeting straight after the session, but by the time I arrived and sat down, my whole ear was throbbing.

And that's the funny thing: although I now had a deformed ear, and now possibly for life, I was also quite proud to have a war medal.

There's no doubt that anyone who has a cauliflower ear has earned it, simply by dint of taking an abrasive beatdown. Before, I had looked at white belts with terrible ears and thought: "God, I'd hate that to happen to me. I'd have ruined ears and still not be able to fight."

Now, though, my thinking was: sod it. I may not be able to have a proper fight like most decent Jiu-Jitsu players, but compared to those just starting, I can often dominate them.

It felt like my cauliflower ear was the fifth stripe on my white belt.

Iit was like the Jiu-Jitsu gods were saying to me: "We won't let you pass through onto blue belt unless you sacrifice an ear." Because really, that's what it is.

There's a saying you hear boxers use, which is: "If you step in the shower, you're going to get wet." They say this in defence of journalists who might ask them why they got hit so many times in their last fight.

But it's a good analogy regarding ears and Jiu-Jitsu, too. Your ears are going to get mashed up in most cases. Of course they are. It's like seeing a boxer with a perfectly straight nose despite taking thousands of punches to his face over the course of his career. They're not going to have a straight nose.

Equally, if you spend up to ten hours a week having men of all weights grinding their hips over your head and folding your ears back accidentally as they try to choke you out with their limbs, it's pretty unlikely that you're going to end up with a glittering career as an ear model.

Curiously though, I have met plenty of decent Jiu-Jitsu fighters whose ears are still intact. If you met them in the street, you'd have no idea that they were a black belt in Jiu-Jitsu. 'How could that be?' I'd often wonder. But it just is what it is. Some experienced BJJ fighters don't have terrible-looking ears and I have no idea why. For most people, Jiu-Jitsu demands that you metaphorically cut an ear off and post it to the Goddess of Jiu-Jitsu, to show her your love. But for some of these fighters, their ears are just fine.

However when I showed my right ear to my wife, she suggested I see a doctor immediately to get it drained.

And so, after deliberating about whether we could just buy some syringes off Amazon and get her to do — "Oh, you're a bloody idiot," the look on my wife's face seemed to say — I finally booked an appointment to see the doctor.

The doctor in turn waved off my story about how maybe my wife could have done it because I'd seen guys in the gym syringe the blood out of each other's ears a few times (check out the horror videos on YouTube for some maximum 'holy shit' moments).

Instead, the doctor pointed me straight in the direction of the hospital.

CHAPTER FOURTEEN

I'm glad that I listened to both my wife and the doctor. Because when I explained to the ear specialist at the hospital that, hey, you know, I've seen guys drain the blood from each other's newly developed cauliflower ears all the time, he just frowned at me disapprovingly.

"Why not?" I asked.

"Because firstly, if you do it, bacteria can get into the ear and cause all kinds of complications. Which is why I'm giving you penicillin antibiotics to fight against an infection. And secondly, because if you withdraw blood from the ear but you don't reshape it with a piece of tough cotton around it, then the cartilage will become like jelly."

"My ear will become like jelly!?"

I recoiled in disgust, at the same time thinking about all the guys down the gym with ears that do look a bit jelly-ish.

"Jelly," he said.

And then my mind flitted to a previous week when I'd been on a work trip, saw that there was a BJJ gym nearby and so had dropped in to see if I could do a pay-as-you-go class.

And the guy at the reception did genuinely have the most squishy, jelly-like ears I'd ever seen.

After nearly two years of Jiu-Jitsu, though, I still wasn't prepared for how squishy this guy's ears were. As he was talking to me, all I could think was: 1) holy cow, those are some properly squishy ears; and 2) this guy has totally gone all in with his BJJ! His ears are like bendy rubber!

He was a very polite guy, and I was grateful for his courtesy. But when you meet a guy like that with such rubber ears, all you can think is, 'Respect, for giving your only set of ears to the sport.'

Maybe it's a rite of passage thing, but as the doctor sterilised my ear, all I could think was that by having a properly dodgy ear, maybe I was finally living the life of someone tougher than the man-child I'd always considered myself to be.

And then the doctor took out the scalpel and handed it to his junior doctor, who, just as an aside, had the world's biggest mole I'd ever seen on the end of her nose. "Why don't you just have it cut it off?" I wanted to shout. "You're a doctor. You're so bright. You're charming. You're educated. You're kind. What the hell is that thing on your nose for? Get it off. You've got it all to play for!"

"Right, doc?!" I imagined saying, looking at the doctor in front of me. "Right? Why are you doing this to yourself?"

I then noticed the wedding ring and thought, Jesus. At what point in the courting process did the other half reference that thing? Or maybe it was true love. Maybe it really was true love. She had her mole. I had my cauliflower ear. Maybe her mole was a lesson from history for me, but a good one. Like, even with my dodgy ear, my wife still might love me.

Yet my imaginary conversation with the doctor about that nose mole fell on imaginary deaf ears.

Instead, my mind focused back on the scene at hand. As the senior doctor pulled out a scalpel, I gripped the wooden handles of my seat.

"We're going to slice part of your ear and let the blood pour out," the doctor said.

"What?"

"Yes," he said, handing the scalpel to his colleague. "But first we need to inject your ear with a painkiller."

A needle was pulled out, and I gripped the seat harder, gritted my teeth, kept my lips wide and started breathing heavily through my teeth. "*Wow*, I'm an insane weakling!" I thought.

The needle went in, straight into what felt like the swollen part of my ear. I started tensing up badly. I tried to imagine what it must be like to be tortured as a prisoner of war. And I was ashamed that I was now literally sweating over a tiny needle being injected into my ear. It bloody hurt though.

And then a female nurse bursts in and starts telling both doctors about someone who's just come into A&E.
"He can't see and he can't talk," she says breathlessly, as both doctors pivot around to stare at this nurse.

And yet, as much as I want to hear all about this person who can't breathe and find out what the hell is going on out there — is the guy ok?! — I can't. Why? Because the junior doctor has just picked up a scalpel and is moving closer towards me, mid-conversation, multitasking between cutting open my ear and finding out more vital information about the man that's just entered A&E..

I start imagining how it must feel to have your nails pulled out by torturers to make you give up state secrets, before killing you and then dumping your body in a landfill.

Holy shit. I'm losing my mind. It's just a bloody scalpel.
"Excuse me?" I ask. "Can you please tell me what exactly you're going to do with that scalpel?"
"Well," says the senior doctor. "We're going to — "
"He's about 80, this poor man," the nurse chimes in, still talking about the injured man who's just come in. "Apparently, he's — "
"WILL YOU FUCKING SHUT UP?" I want to scream at the nurse. I'm shitting my pants here. They're going to stick that scalpel in my head or something. I need some details. I'm very sorry about the old man, but...

Oh gosh, both doctors are now right up next to me, the junior doctor raising the scalpel. I grit my teeth again, and start breathing heavily through the front of my head, trying to pull in air through any orifice in my face I can. I'm grimacing, and tensing my whole body up, a bit like you do when you're walking down the street and you suddenly get so struck down by the urge to do a poo that if you don't find a public toilet soon it'll charge out of your bottom and into your pants with the super-sonic heat of a rocket.
"Are you okay, love?" the nurse says to me, now totally forgetting about the poor bastard she was just describing who couldn't see or speak. "Was it a rugby injury?"

I ignore her, because if I look at her, I'll probably start crying with self-pity. I think of the film, Marathon Man, with Dustin Hoffman, where some lunatic Nazi dentist rips out his teeth without anaesthetic.

God. In spite of my doing so much Jiu-Jitsu that I've not got a cauliflower ear, I'm profoundly disturbed by my own cowardice. The senior doctor looks at me to explain what's happening but I can't really see him as he's looking down at me with a bright light behind him, as if he's an angel with a weapon, in order that his colleague will be able to cut into my ear precisely.

I feel a sharp spike in my ear, and can feel warm blood pumping down the side of my neck. Am I dying? DOC, TELL ME THE TRUTH? AM I DYING? He's basically just popped the swelling on the side of my ear like it's a balloon filled with water.

The blood keeps pouring until his colleague sucks it up with a small suction tube similar to the ones you see at the dentist.

He then places a piece of rolled up cotton around the inside of the ear so that it can remould into its usual circular shape around the top. Together they then wrap a bandage around my head to maintain pressure on the ear. Their goal is to stop the ear refilling again.

And that's it.

I look like a member of the walking wounded. Only with the world's most pathetic injury. Still. I'm thrilled. I'm almost fixed, I think.

"How soon until I can go back to Jiu-Jitsu?" I ask.

"Well, what do you care about more, your ear or Jiu-Jitsu?" the doctor asks.

And for about 15 seconds I'm not sure how to answer. Actually, I'm still not.

"Wait five days and then you can exercise again," I'm told.

But by Day Four, it gets too much. I want to train. That evening I drive to the gym...

Of course, I should have waited. But then I was thinking of

everyone I'd ever seen who was good at the sport. They all had ruined ears. And then I compared it to a sport like boxing, and thought: unlike boxing, it's not damaging my brain.

So if ruining the shape of my ears in some way to the sport is the only sacrifice I'd have to make, then that's the sacrifice I'd have to make, I told myself. It also reminded me that once you get a cauliflower ear, and it's really bad, basically there's no going back to your old life of not doing Jiu-Jitsu. Otherwise you've just disfigured your ears for nothing. So you may as well double-down.

That said, the experience with my cauliflower ear wasn't quite finished yet. Although I'd accepted that the ear would keep filling with blood and become bulbous again until I completely stopped doing Jiu-Jitsu, at which point the doctors said the blood would potentially just drain back into my body, I really didn't expect what happened next.

While rolling with a heavy guy one evening, the instructor told us to stop.
"You're bleeding," he said, pointing to the side of his head to indicate that I may have cut my temple.
"Hmm," I thought, "I can't feel any blood or cuts on my head."
I got some toilet roll and went to have a look.

It turned out that under the weight of the guy rolling around with me, my cauliflower ear had taken too much pressure. After immediately refilling with blood again a day after I'd had my ear dressing taken off, the ear could take no more abrasion. It had been virtually bursting with blood.

And now it had popped.

Blood continued to trickle down my neck.

And yet it was bitter sweet. The fact that my cauliflower ear had actually popped was a blessing.
It made the swelling come right down, only refilling slightly overnight.

And then, while sparring again a few days later, I took yet another few knocks on that ear and it swelled up, this time even bigger than before.

I would now need corrective surgery to fix my ear should I ever feel the need to return my ear to how it looked before.

And yet I couldn't blame Jocko, the podcaster whose enthusiasm for BJJ got me into the sport. My gratitude vastly outweighed my dismay. Jocko wasn't to blame for my damaged ear any more than lifting weights was to blame for callused palms.

But my subconscious had other ideas. Despite having thought that I'd come to terms with my cauliflower ear, I nevertheless woke up one morning having had one of the most peculiar dreams of my life.

In the dream, I'd gone on a mission to kill Jocko.

I don't know why I was on the mission, perhaps it was my subconscious trying to punish him for my ear. But I'd had faith in my abilities to kill him. Accompanied by two Navy Seals, who unlike Jocko, had a blackness to them, a poverty to their souls, we met in a dingy, dimly lit, brown-hued hotel room in a grimy city somewhere.

But once on our mission, I recall us creeping around this huge white holiday mansion.

Through the palm trees, I remember looking up at him on the balcony where he was stood, topless, talking to his wife. Here it was. My big moment in the dream. I'd had the option to act.

But, scared that I'd upset his wife nearby and equally scared that he'd hear me and do me in first, I continued to skirt around the undergrowth of this pristine villa that looked like something Pablo Escobar might have lived in.

And when I got back to the grimy hotel, I couldn't understand why I hadn't acted.

When I woke from my dream, I was equally bemused. Just what the hell had that dream been about?

And yet, while walking to work and reflecting on it, I think I knew the answer.

I was angry with Jocko for getting me my cauliflower ear. I blamed him. His advice meant I now had a comedy right ear. And there he was in his fancy mansion. And there I was in my grimy nondescript life, surrounded by my confused ideals of heroism.

And so I'd gone to punish my mentor Jocko. And when I'd seen him up close, he was topless, half-naked. Exposed. Just a human. And yet he was still terrifying in his toplessness. As if my subconscious was saying, "He's no perfect physical specimen. And neither are you. But don't kill the value you gave Jocko in your life. He gave you Jiu-Jitsu. And for that alone — as well as the fact that if he'd heard me crawling around his home in my dream he would have killed me — for that alone, it's not quite time to murder your idols. Keep Jocko as one mental source to pull on in life, as he's served you well," my brain seemed to be saying.

"He has his place in that huge white mansion. He's earned it. At the same time," I reflected, "it's time to also leave him in that world. You've learnt what you can from him. But now you must become your own man."

And so, with my gammy ear, and with gratitude to Jocko, that's just what I did. Jocko had gotten me almost all the way through white belt. But now I had to move forwards on my own terms.

CHAPTER FIFTEEN

As my right ear continued to swell, though, I did discover within me a newfound reluctance about my BJJ journey. But it wasn't just my comedy ear that was giving me jip. I also experienced a new feeling about the sport in general from within myself. The closer I got to blue belt, it seemed, with guys at the gym saying, "Not long now until you get your blue belt," all I could think of was the knackering two years it had taken me to get this far.

I realised how slowly the body learns to fight the BJJ way, even for fast learners. Just to be able to know how to maintain a decent level of control over your opponent takes years.

And with only the prospect of having gotten to nearly blue belt after so much hard sweating now weighing heavily on me, I did begin to think that maybe I needed to take a brief holiday from it.

Maybe I'd had enough. Not forever. Just for a period of time.

The problem with Jiu-Jitsu is that to stop training every day is to very quickly see your physical fitness and flexibility diminish. You can instantly tell the difference between a person who rolls six days a week and someone who only rolls twice. They're light years apart in terms of fitness and skill set, calmness under pressure and physical agility. And I preferred to be the six times a week guy. So now, although I fancied a little break, I felt trapped.

Because I also knew that one week off would turn into ten days which would turn into a month and then three months. And soon it would be like I'd never done BJJ at all. I would become just some guy with an ugly ear who couldn't fight. So I'd be exactly where I was when I'd started Jiu-Jitsu only now with a horrid ear.

So I decided to just keep going.

And for about a week, that seemed like a good idea. It felt like I'd been brave enough to carry on regardless, that I'd overcome my demons.

Until my ear suddenly became ginormous again. I'd been rolling with a very good blue belt and although I'd put up the best fight possible — trying to close the distance all the time between my belt line and his, for example — there was just no way around it. He was dominating me again. And again. And again. Tap. Reset. Tap. Reset. Tap. In the end I was practically getting repetitive strain injury in both wrists just from tapping.

But at least I was wearing my ear guards, I thought. Sure, the guy I was sparring was rough. But my right ear had been cut open and bled out a week ago. What with the time lapse between the blood being let out of my ear, and the fact that I was wearing ear guards, I thought I'd be fine. But in the excitement of sparring, the sheer fun and thrill of it, my ear guards came away at the Velcro and fell apart down the middle.

Too engaged with the sparring, and frustrated by the repetitive faff of having to put them back together, I just kept rolling. I felt my right ear get banged a bit but it was no big deal. I'd be fine.

Two days later, and my right ear was full. Where once there had been a large amount of puffiness now there was just a swollen bulbous blob with a hole in where my ear had allegedly once been.

On the Monday I was due to start work at a new job and the last thing I wanted to do was turn up like Mr. Bump from The Mr. Men Show. So instead of going back to the hospital, I just tolerated it and checked in at the new office to my first day of work.

The lady from HR greeted me in that perfectly polished way HR people know how to in order to avoid any opportunity whatsoever of getting the company sued.

But despite her best efforts to be warm and yet corporate, I kept noticing her eyes move ever so slightly towards my right ear.

I later checked it in the work toilets mirror and it really had grown. In fact it was growing so much that I wondered at what point it would stop swelling.

I was also torn. Although it's important to get cauliflower ears looked at and mended ASAP before the blood hardens in them permanently, and you're left disfigured for life, I also knew that taking a day off to sit in A&E to get my ear cut open again wasn't exactly a strong look on your first week of a new job. Plus I didn't want to draw attention to myself by then coming back to the office with a massive bandage bound around my head.

By the Saturday, though, I looked ridiculous. My whole ear was engorged with blood. I had the ears of Conor McGregor but the fighting skills of Ewan McGregor. And so I felt like a fraud; like a fake hard man. When my puffy blood-filled ear had popped while rolling the first time around, my instructor had wrapped some white finger tape around a hard piece of toilet roll in order to hold the bleeding in place, adding, "Now you look hard..."

"Yes, but I'm a white belt," I replied.

"Well, at least you look the part..." he smiled, kindly.

And he was right. I did look the part. The only problem was that I didn't feel the part. After nearly two years of driving to the academy, I'd still always get a slight tingle in my stomach from nerves every time I pulled up near the gym. I was still scared of fighting.

Ultimately when the Sunday rolled around, I decided to skip Jiu-Jitsu (despite panicking that it would have meant I'd only trained three times that week, which was lousy), and I headed to the hospital.

This time it felt like old hat. I checked in with the nurse, who passed me on to the doctor, a new one, who listened politely to what happened to my ear and then blew his cheeks as I spoke.

"Will I have to get my ear tied to my head with a really tight bandage again? I've just gotten a new job."

"Hmm," he said. He looked at my right ear. Okay, he decided. He was going to get a needle and try to suck the blood out.

And then in the doctor went with the needle.

"A small scratch," he said, preparing me for imminent pain with a massive lie.

He stuck the needle in, and it hurt.

I gritted my teeth like I did the first time, while at the same time breathing in and out erratically.

I felt a consistent pain for about 15 seconds. And then he pulled the syringe out.

He showed it to me — "Look, two millimetres of blood."

It didn't seem like a lot, though. Certainly not enough to give me the kind of pain I'd just experienced.

"You'd be surprised. That's quite a lot."

I did feel like my ear had less pressure in it.

"But we need to go again," he stressed. "I haven't been able to get all the blood out."

And so, with my hands clasped together and sweating, he stuck in a new needle again. Bloody hell! A small scratch?

I tried to be manly. What would Jocko do?

Nope. Channelling Jocko wasn't working either. I grinned some more while the doctor hurt my ear.

He got more blood out, but he still wasn't satisfied.

I stood up to look in the mirror and was amazed by how less puffy my ear was. It was the difference between a bouncy castle and one that's been deflated.

Yes, the ear was still partly full of blood but only in a relatively minor way.

"I never thought I'd see my ear again," I mumbled, pathetically..

The doctor nodded but he wasn't finished.

"I'm afraid we're going to have to use a scalpel. There's still some blood in there and the only way I'm going to get it out is by slicing it open."

And so, as before, the doctor took out another needle, filled it with anaesthetic, then jabbed that bastard in my ear.

I was now used to getting my ear injected with painkiller so although I was in pain, I realised it wasn't the end of the world.

Until he got busy with his scalpel.

To make sure my ear had numbed seconds later, he began

gently stabbing it with that pointy instrument.

"Can you feel that?" he asked, as he then prodded various parts of my ear with the tip of it with me experiencing varying degrees of pain.

"A bit, yes. No, not that bit. Ow, flipping hell, yes. I'm still a bit tender there."

With him happy that the ear was numb, all I could now feel was some tugging.

But although the sensation in my ear had been numbed, I still obviously had my hearing. So although I was no longer in pain, what was putting me off was the scrat-scrat-scratting noise of the scalpel slicing and pulling and tugging into my ear. It was gross. I was being cut open and all I could hear (but suddenly not feel) was sharp scalpel cutting flesh and letting out blood.

But because the doctor had already extracted quite a lot of red plasma, I was saved from the sensation of gushing blood like last time. It bled out, he mopped me up, then bandaged my head, telling me to come back the following week to have more blood let out of the ear, to release the pressure.

What that meant though for the bigger picture was yet another week off Jiu-Jitsu.

Which in my world meant inevitable 'blobby time'.

Soon, in a matter of days, I inevitably began piling on the weight, and looked like it was me, but in a fat suit. So now I had a gammy ear, a cracking pair of man tits and I wasn't letting off any steam getting crushed into a sweaty mess at Jiu-Jitsu.

I began to panic and feel what little hardness of conditioning I had seep out of me.

I'd still automatically size up every big bloke I saw, to see how I'd defend myself against someone of that size, except now I'd be thinking, "Maybe he could beat the crap out of me after all."

I felt like a White Belt version of Superman when he lost all his powers in the films and comics and was suddenly reduced to his alter ego, Clark Kent. Only in my case, shorter, fatter and shitter. And with male pattern balding. Hello, Ladies!

Not that I was a superman, of course. But I was as goddamn close as I've ever been to my own version of Nietzsche's Superman.

On the mats I was the best me.

Also when life felt like it was dragging me backwards, or my personal life got too crap, or I started asking all the big questions about my purpose in the cosmos, Jiu-Jitsu was like a judge watching my performance and raising a scorecard that just read, "Will you shut up?"

Jiu-Jitsu was like taking yourself outside for 'a straightener' with the negative version of yourself, much like the big fight sequence in the scrapyard in Superman III. And 'Jiu-Jitsu You' always wins. Not because you can sort of fight now but because Jiu-Jitsu is an antidote to the kryptonite of life. Kryptonite's kryptonite is BJJ. It makes you soar when life makes you sore. Jiu-Jitsu really is that special. It helps you breathe.

BUT...There was no question I was losing that power and positivity with my enforced lay-off just to salvage my ear.

I gave it a week, had a fairly shitty time where all I had to look forward to was struggling through work, commuting home, ironing tomorrow's work shirt, and then doing it all again.

And I said to myself, basically, screw my ear. It's a small price to pay when the thrill and endorphins of Jiu-Jitsu is the only stitching keeping you together. I swear: if you're circling the drain in life, and asking the Big Questions (like, 'should I really have a big jacket potato for lunch if my toilet's blocked"), and you're still not settling on an answer, then the sweat, thought and controlled fury of Jiu-Jitsu will set you free.

So, if getting a damaged ear that people couldn't stop wincing at was the price I had to pay to beat Life, who seemed to be punishing me for finding an antidote to its sadness and stress, then forget my ear aesthetics. Let's just get back to the mats!

And so, I signed up for another competition.

If my first competition had been me testing the waters of inter-BJJ club contests, then this time I was going to go at it

fully fledged. I was going to bring the storm.

Okay, I was going to bring a light shower with perhaps a chance of sunshine.

But as rolling with this massively big guy in the gym had told me, Jiu-Jitsu is like Forrest Gump's box of chocolates. You quite literally don't know what you're going to get until the roll is on.

It's not as simple as, 'That guy is massive so he's going to smash me.'

Jiu-Jitsu is a battle of minds, of who can do the most technical thing right now in this moment. What's the most thoughtful thing you can do right now to inch your way towards taking their back, where they've got the lowest chance possible of defending your choke?

Because when you're behind them attacking their back, they just can't see what you're doing. And as long as you're tucked in extremely tight around them, the what-ifs going through their minds become unbearable. I CAN'T SEE! I CAN'T SEE!!

And so that's what I'd do at this next contest. I'd try to take their backs and see if I could choke them out.

CHAPTER SIXTEEN

On a Saturday morning, I nervously pack my bag and head out to the English BJJ Open, the most revered GI (in other words, kimono-based) tournament in the UK.

I try to block out my nerves by doing work on the train to the event in South London. I watch some comedy on pre-downloaded videos on my phone's YouTube app.

But although my favourite comedians are riffing about, "Is it just me, or...", and, "Hello, Milton Keynes, does anyone here come from New Zealand?" all I can think is: bloody hell. This is a high-level competition I'm going to. Therefore I'm certain that the competition will be fierce.

I disembark from the train with my big sports bag, with two kimonos inside, just in case I'm made to wait a long time between my first fight and my possible second fight — I don't want to get cold, after all. My nerves have already put me at a disadvantage.

Ok... The real reason I packed two gi's was in case I did something by mistake, like wee or poo myself. There's the truth. You have it. This hasn't happened before. But nothing would end my chances of success quite like pooing myself by accident. So, just in case I were to accidentally fill my trousers during a bout, I packed two gi's.

Now approaching the university sports hall where the event is being held, I'm again taken aback by how normal — although quite tall and physically strong — the other people walking towards the entrance look. Again, I'm reminded that you really cannot tell who is competent at grappling these days just by looking at them, and that's the beauty of Jiu-Jitsu. No facial marks are left like they are with striking sports like boxing, s you just can't tell who does it.

The closer I get to the sports hall, the more people I see leaving it, having just had their bouts, win, lose or draw.

And in most cases, it's parents my age with their children. Their kids have just fought. They're wearing medals and holding certificates citing their placements within the top three places: gold, silver or bronze.

And all I can think is: Jesus... these kids are so small. Do they know what they've just done? They've had a fight and survived. And yet, they're so tiny compared to me. They're six years old, or younger! And here I am, a grown-up 40-year-old man who could easily be their dad. And I'm bricking it!

As I walk past these parents with their kids in their big, floppy, white martial arts outfits, with their winter coats over them to keep them warm, I catch dads and mums chatting to their little boys and girls about where they went right and wrong in their fights, and it's heart-breaking. More so because that warmth and humanity is at such odds with the complete sense of terror stirring within me.

Entering the building, I walk up the long corridor towards the hall, say hello in passing to a few people I recognise from other gyms, and sit down at a table at a cafe seating area divided off from the hall by a large wall of plastic glass.

I'm three hours early, and so I'm faced with the dilemma of walking through into the melee of the hall, with a bout taking place every five minutes on each of the six mats.

But now I'm utterly terrified by what awaits me. I peer through the glass to see people of all ages chatting lightly or animatedly, but rarely with anger.

No one here is aggravated. Instead it's just people fighting on mats or watching their teammates and loved ones fight for the honour of being called 'The English Champion' in their weight category.

More kids and teenagers walk past me, followed by all kinds of adults of various shapes and sizes. Some are darting to changing rooms to get ready for their fights, while others are sat at tables just chatting.

I do want to go into the hall where all the fights are taking place to soak up the atmosphere but I'm just not ready for it.

I sit outside, fiddle with my phone, then try to put my face in my forearms on a table and get some sleep. It doesn't work.

The waiting and over-thinking is exhausting me.

In my head, I start to rationalise the bravery of everyone here younger than me. "It's okay for the kids to all fight — no wonder they're not scared. They're all so tiny, so how exactly can they get hurt?! They know this. That's why all the youngsters here are so chilled...."

And then I remember my childhood and how utterly consumed by fear I was, and how most kids are also at the prospect of having a fight. I recall my tearful attempts to defend myself in my best mate's bedroom as a kid, before getting picked up by my todger and nipples.

"What am I talking about?" I think.

If anything, it's scarier to fight as a child than it is as an adult. When you're a kid, the world is a vengeful hierarchy without any laws. If you get beaten up and snitch, you're a grass. If you can't defend yourself, you get pummelled. And humiliated. And if you tell your parents to step in and help you to stop getting bullied, you hate yourself and everything you stand for, for being so weak.

When you're a grown-up though, you take your concept of having rights and the rule of law to heart. This is a democracy. There are jails. The law is taken very seriously. Hit someone and it's prison, as I had tried to cowardly convince myself all those moons ago when I'd nearly been beaten up by that big guy outside the underground after he'd charged into the bag I'd been carrying.

Yet in a Jiu-Jitsu tournament, I realised now, your opponent may go hard, but at least you know your very existence isn't on the line. Reason will prevail.

Which isn't the case when you're a kid. You have no idea as a youngster about how the system works. And for that reason alone, I decided, the kids deserve more props than the adults. If it's scary for the grown-ups, it must be mortifying for the kids.

So I tell myself to shut up and enter the hall to take a look around.

Ahead of me, I see a teammate in the middle of his fight on the mats, surrounded by at least two hundred onlookers. He's winning and dominating the guy.

Amidst the faces of spectators screaming for their man to win, I also notice plenty of red-faced people — either fighters who've just finished their bouts and they're looking tired and sweaty but elated, or fighters like me who are just walking around, shitting their pants in anticipation of their upcoming match.

Screw this, I tell myself. I need to get into the mind-set and get ready for my fight. Few things are most exhausting than waiting around for a big event to happen and thinking, 'What if?'

And so, I head to the changing rooms and get changed into my gi, before being ripped out of my competitive mind-set by the panicking thought that I still don't really know how to tie my white belt yet. I've tried to do it plenty of times by now, but I'm still not sure how to do it. It's the perfect metaphor for my own Jiu-Jitsu ability. I can't even tie my own belt, I think.

I look around at all the other white belts walking past, and they too haven't really mastered this complicated knack; their belts are all bunched up and unkempt around their waists.

I quickly try to snap out of all of my daft, high-minded personal analysis and just crack on with getting my head straight. I try to get into the mind of a fighter. Although my bum cheeks are flapping like nobody's business, I say to myself, "Act like a Terminator robot that will not stop until its mission is complete. DO NORMAL FACE, LIKE JOCKO SAYS! And maybe go to the toilet in a minute. Just in case."

Yet although I'm now walking around the hall amongst the six matches around me, looking like I've got a tragic muscular problem with my face that prevents me from making facial expressions, I just can't stop wondering whether I might just have a mind-blank in there while fighting and forget every single thing that I've learnt. So I have a private word with myself:

"Just get in there and think, 'Right, what's the most technical thing I can do right now?' That's all you have to do. Don't think about moves. Just think technical! Technical! Technical! And that should give your mind exactly the right thing to focus on, in itself blocking out all your mind's negative chatter.'"

So that's what I did. I would think "technical" and just hang onto that mantra as my lifeline throughout my fight.

I get called to my mat to fight, and get weighed in — at 89 kilos, I'm 5 kilos (in other words: 11 pounds; or nearly a stone) under the cut-off for my bracket, heavyweight. Which means that the guys I'm about to be fighting will have quite a large weight advantage over me.

"But that's fine," I tell myself. "I want to fight heavy guys — the big guys. It's the big guys I've always been scared of, after all."

"Plus," I remember, "Jiu-Jitsu is about technique, not power. In the end, technique beats power (unless your opponent has both!)"

I then make my way towards the mat, and watch the match before mine is due unfold.

Two guys are throwing each other around violently; a bald guy who looks like Blofeld from James Bond, and a man who looks like Will Ferrell. They're going total gang-busters on one another.

I look at my gi, the same one that one of the competitors in front of me is wearing, and I wonder if I'd cope if I was now in his place, fighting his opponent, under that violent pressure.

With both of us being bald and both wearing the same branded outfit, I wonder if the fact he's being splatted all over the mat is a foreshadowing of what's about to happen to me.

Back on the mat, in fact, my doppelgänger is now bleeding from his eyebrow.

The referee stops the fight, and the medic comes over, puts a plaster over his eye, and they restart their bout, only for my doppelgänger to get submitted by his opponent.

It's a reminder that although Jiu-Jitsu is safe as a sport, it's very rough and tumble.

I look to my left and see another guy waiting for his fight. He's got thick hair, a massive beard, he's tall, and he's a lump.

Jesus, I think. Please say that isn't my opponent. Please, God. He's massive. Strong.

"Hi, hello — are you Ben?"

A right hand is held out from my left hand side towards me. I turn around. He introduces himself as my opponent, and I'm instantly relieved. The hairy lump must be waiting by the mats to fight in the weight division above, the ultra-heavyweights.

I shake hands with my forthcoming opponent.

"I'm so nervous," he says. "So nervous."

He's a man in his late thirties whose boyish truth is heartwarming and endearing. But I won't let myself soften until after we've fought. He might be an absolute monster, I decide.

So I try to win the psychological advantage by saying very little.

Rudely, I just grunt back. I then edge away from him, in the hope that his confidence drains some more. If I connect with him on a human level, it'll drain me back down to my normal humanity and I'll start talking to him about all my usual nonsense — and the ability to actually have the will to fight him will vanish.

So I give him nothing back. Cruelly, I sense his invisible antenna retract slowly back into his mind. We'll make friends after. But though I'm not great at Jiu-Jitsu, I came here to try my hardest and win.

After watching the big hairy guy have his fight, which is just a vicious, mad scramble of limbs that he wins, we're called to the mats.

Shit, this is it. The English Open Championships.

We get ushered towards the ref in the centre of the mat, shake his hand, shake hands with each other, then the ref chops the air between us.

And we're off.

I can feel my inner strength drain out from my body, like invisible dysentery. Just the anticipation of this moment of impact has exhausted me through worry. But now I'm here.

I remember Jocko's 'normal face' advice to all his podcast listeners. Scared? Just pull your normal face — and all that fear will dissipate. So that's what I do, and it works.

My opponent charges forward, and I'm amazed at the wide expanse of his back as his head hooks under my right armpit.

He's hit me in the sternum with his bulk and we fall to the floor. He's scrambling all over me, but I hold it together by telling myself, "Ok, fine, he's done that, and sure, I'm absolutely soiling my gi trousers right now, but still: what's the most technical thing I can do now...and now...and now...?"
And to my amazement, it works. By actually using my brain to slow the fight down and think, I begin using technique and dictating the pace that I want to fight at. I'm using my brain to fight my way out of hell.

I may be in the English Open's lair, but in this moment, in the middle of my white belt fight, it's now on my terms. It's up to me to control this experience so that I come out on top.

I sit up, but my opponent is leaning into me. I scoop my left arm around his neck, and grab the flesh of my left hand with my right. I then thrust the blade of my wrist, the sharp part, up into his neck, as per the traditional guillotine move. It's almost on, and choking him, but he's powerful and is wriggling and thrashing about at me like a deer with its neck trapped in a fence.

I realise this could be my moment, and hook my left leg under his right leg, while pushing off on the ground with my right foot. He flies up and over me in the air while I've still got his head in my guillotine. I'm now on top of him, almost exactly in the way I was during my very first fight, at my first and only tournament up till now..

He has my full bodyweight on him now, plus I'm choking him from above. He needs to tap before his head pops off. But he won't because he's proud.

And in that moment, I pause in my own head for a second and cut away to a very truthful, uncomfortable realisation about my own dark side.

While I'm in this fight, and choking him, all I have is primal bloodlust running through me. And it's both thrilling and absolutely shameful.

And I know I'm not alone in feeling these kinds of sensations. In the gym, when you get tapped out by people, in their eyes you see satisfaction and pride — their own sense that they've just owned and dominated you — their animalistic, predatory senses that we all have, lightly smattered with a sense of human empathy.

They've 'killed' you, as it were, and overpowered and outthought and man-handled you in a way that's like an injection of self-belief into their soul. For that instant, they consider themselves to be a more advanced human, a more skilful fighter, and better able to defend their tribe than you are. And they're right. If the end point of a failed civilisation is extreme self-defence, then when the talking is done, this is what it often comes down to: violence.

The good news is, once you get tapped, there's a rush of humanity that almost immediately floods the brain of most people who've just tapped you.

They've also been tapped many, many, many times before, and it's a wake-up call to a person's illusory sense of self-worth. Getting tapped is the ultimate reckoning. And yet, at the same time, you're having fun — and it's no big deal at all.

Jiu-Jitsu: honestly, it's got the whole human experience rolled into one. As the saying goes, "If coffee and Jiu-Jitsu can't fix you, nothing will."

My opponent beneath me taps — a mind-boggling thought given how fearful of violence I've been throughout my life. And I then have my usual mini-panic that I haven't been quick enough to let go of the person tapping in case they're actually, genuinely hurt.

The poor guy lies on his back as the referee separates us, squeezes his eyes shut and groans in both a need to get his breath back and also in disappointment that he's just been beaten.

I tenderly tap him on the shoulder as we stand up and we

embrace like good friends. Together we've shared an unforgettable experience that I genuinely feel can go in the 'Plus' column of events in your life that make you a better person. That's just how fighting someone and yet having no ill feelings towards them feels. It's a sense of respect shared between two strangers expressing themselves through a sport that's captured their imagination.

The referee raises my hand, and I hear my teammates cheer. But I try not to get too excited. I've still got the Final to face.

I stand by the edge of the mat, waiting for my next fight. I'm happy, but now nervous. This is for the gold, for the honour of being able to call myself English Champion, which seems ridiculous really as I basically know practically nothing, even though I just managed to tap someone.

Okay, I tell myself. I need to make this next five-minute fight the most important five minutes of my life. I need to think about everything I'm doing at every minute. I need to be technical.

But then I'm haunted by that same voice I heard when I was at my first tournament, before my final fight, where I was beaten and didn't get the gold: "You've got silver. You're on the podium," my internal voice was saying to me. "That's good enough, isn't it?"

No, it's not, I remind myself. You're here to win. Yes, I'm not great at this sport, but I do have four-stripes on my white belt. "You're nearly a blue belt," I shout back at my inner voice. "You need to win. You've put in all that work, you idiot. Yes, you're still terrible at this sport, but it's all relative — your opponents are also not that great either by dint of them being white belts! So get out there and win!"

And yet the voice of negativity continued flooding my mind: "Yeah, but it doesn't really matter if you win. You don't need the gold. Look at all the other people you know who've won gold before at their tournaments. How did it change their life? They're still them, just like you'll still be you if you lose. You've got silver. YOU GOT SILVER!"

Snapping back into the present, I stand there on the edge of the mats, and I can't believe my mind is being so cowardly. I thought I was better than this.

I'm trying to do Jocko's 'Normal Face' but the fear keeps bursting through. Bloody hell, I'm crapping myself. I think I'm just going to start throwing up.

And then, that big hairy guy who I'd been convinced must have fought in the ultra-heavyweight division walks past me, slightly too close to my personal space, and then on towards his spectating wife and child to speak to them. I feel my heart beats flutter so close together like a butterfly panicking; an odd sensation that leaves me feeling light-headed, adrenalised, and also as if I've got an entire building resting on my chest.

Oh, bloody hell. He's not ultra-heavy, after all. He's in my division. Jesus: I've got to fight him for the gold...

My mind starts Rolodexing through all the men I've been confronted by throughout my life. In almost every situation, it's involved me looking up at someone in fear, and never looking down at someone else. I've always been the nail to their overbearing hammers.

Maybe there's some psychological advantage of looking down on someone to the extent that it makes you feel less scared, and more in control.

But whenever I've worried about what's going to happen next, it almost always involved cranking my head to look upwards.

Yet the human truth of the matter is that few people pick a fight with someone bigger than them. That's why I've always looked up in fear instead of down.

Big people know they're big, and that must be a nice feeling.

Yet here I am, supposedly about to have the toughest fight of my life, and yet I'm feeling all my life-source drain out through my legs and into the ground.

What the hell is happening to me?

We're both called to the centre of the mat.

I stand opposite this Goliath, and I'm instantly giving him the psychological advantage. Even though we weigh the same give or take a few kilos, in my mind he's a giant. He's taller, certainly. He's a human Godzilla.

The ref chops the air and we charge at each other. Ok, react, react...

He grabs my right leg and we fall to the ground. I ball up while facing him, legs and arms upwards like a dog that's just died and now got rigor mortis. I don't know what I'm thinking. I'm panicking.

But he's all over me: putting his full bodyweight on me. He's now kneeling on my face and I'm thinking, 'Hold on, is this even legal? Maybe it is. Well, it doesn't really hurt that much, so it must be...'

"No kneeling like that," says the ref to my opponent

I try to do something, trying to take the bull by the horns, but I'm being so roughed up that I can't get my head straight. "What am I supposed to do here? I don't know. What would I do in a sparring session at my club?"

I manage to get his bodyweight off me slightly but I've got no tangible counterattack. I'm not really doing anything anymore, though I'm not sure why. I'm just lying there getting pummelled.

"What the hell am I doing?" I'm thinking, unable to relax. "Do something!"

He gets both of his knees over my body so I'm pinned down, so I bounce him off my slightly by thrusting my hips up, then I shift to my side. He's then on top of me again, digging his right knee into my stomach. Well, that sort of hurts. But again, it's not that bad.

I ball up once more but I'm still facing him, on my back, looking up at him, like a man examining with fascination the perfect symmetry of lines in a brick wall while it simultaneously collapses on him.

Wake up. Wake up. Wake up.

I need to get into this fight. I need to attack!

But do I attack outright or do I counter-attack?

I'm so confused.

I decide to counter attack.

Which is at least better than lying there, like I've fallen asleep under the Sunday papers, and getting crushed.

He grabs my collar and lifts me up by the back of my kimono trousers and I feel a brush of cold.

It now dawns on me that by trying to pick me up by the back of my trousers in order to crush my face with my own knees, my opponent has just ripped my bum cheeks out. My full arse is now naked and staring at the crowd. Around 150 people watching can now see not just my pasty white buttocks but also my full bum crack. If my trousers and accompanying sports underwear were to be pulled up any further towards my head, I realise, it's quite possible that my willy and full giblets would be on show.

Weirdly, unlike in sparring where this has almost happened to me before and I got a bit cagey about getting my bum out in public, in this instance I feel totally at ease about it.

Sure my bum may be on display, but c'est la vie, I realise.

Maybe my opponent will see my bum crack and he'll stop stacking me and tap himself out, I think. Maybe he'll see my bum and retch, providing me with a few valuable moments to counter-attack. I hope I've wiped properly. Is it possible to smell of Hell when you're sweating this heavily? I've noticed that people's individual body odour disappears once they start sweating heavily in sparring. Maybe, like dreadlocks apparently, a sweaty bum cleans itself?

"WILL YOU FUCKING SHUT UP AND START FIGHTING!" I scream at myself, in my head.

But it's wishful thinking. My opponent has got the gold medal on his mind and his wife and toddler in the audience are watching, seeking confirmation that he really is their shield.

No, genuinely, I really must start attacking now, I think.

And so, with both buttocks hanging out, and with me being pummelled underneath his weight, I try to put myself back together again.

This man, like all the other big men I've come up against in life so far, has stolen a part of my soul, not because he planned to necessarily, but because my mind went into panic mode. I saw a big guy before me, and shat myself like I've done since I attained human consciousness and became self-aware.

After all I'd trained, and after coming this far, it seemed, I was still dealing with the demons from my past.

And still, to my incredible disbelief, my mind was saying to me: "Look, maybe you should just give this fight to him," (like I had a choice!). "He's got his wife and daughter here. They're a happy family. Forget all that Jocko crap about bettering yourself. Romance is an enduring idea. Jocko is just one man. But the symmetry of life, a family man winning a gold medal in front of his loving wife and young child, is such a lovely notion. It's pure Hollywood. Maybe I should just ride this fight out...."

And yet against this self-poisoning of my mind, the human voice of me that isn't a coward, that knows he has a dark side like every other human, screamed, "NO! Get in there and be a man."

"But, I'm scared..."

"PRIVATE PILE," I think go myself, channeling the red-faced drill sergeant from the movie, Full Metal Jacket. "YOU ARE A FAT BARREL OF HUMAN TURD, GET IN THERE — AND START SWINGING!!"

Amidst the screaming faces in the crowd I imagine Jocko being stood there, silently, expressionlessly, but also like the spirit of Braveheart's dead wife at the end of the movie, when Mel Gibson's tied to the rack, being stretched, and getting his ball-bag sawed in half by that medieval nutter.

I imagine Jocko looking at me, all quiet, indignant fury underneath a face devoid of emotion, but now slowly pulling a used, bloody axe out from behind his back.

"MURDER HIM!"

The message is clear from the depths of my psyche. Give no inch. Give no quarter. In the words of Jocko, "Go down swinging like a man possessed."

I grab the big hairy man's ankle, push up against his body as it's pushing down on me, and the big hairy dude falls backwards, like the Leaning Tower of Pisa as if its underpinning has perished, no longer able to support its weight.

Sod this, I tell myself. Why should we work together, me and this big guy, to make sure he gets the outcome he wants? We came to fight.

I make a choice. Go home knowing that I just lay there and took a pummelling as this guy gave it all he had and had no mercy on me — or actually stand up for myself.

I'm me at my friend's house getting bullied. I'm me getting knocked and shoulder-barged as an adult on the way to work. I'm the boy at school getting charged into from across the school playground. I'm me as an adult, getting eyeballed up close by a commuting human giant, intimidated by him until I'd yelped, desperately, "I'm calling the police..."

I am every pathetic bloke who's been too scared to stand up for himself, who was too afraid to act in the moment to defend himself, preferring to defer an altercation and instead confront the fear of self-disappointment in his own private time, behind closed doors. I am The Man Who Always Says Sorry.

And this guy I'm fighting literally has his knee back on my face right now, again!

Do I love avoiding confrontation, only to feel terrible about myself later, or am I the guy who'll confront the trouble right now, the consequences be damned, because in this very moment I'm under attack.

Just exactly what kind of man have I become? Who the hell am I? I'm nearly halfway through my life, and really when have I ever stood up and said, Enough!

Instead I carry my individual frustrations around with me like a rucksack stuffed with slices of bitter lemons, my sorrowful recollections of my own moments of weakness strapped to my person.

Well, fuck that and fuck this.

And fuck this otherwise probably very lovely guy trying to do as much damage to me as possible right now within the confines of this competition's rules. (Although I'm pretty sure that pinning my head to the floor by kneeling through my nose isn't in the rule book).

Also who cares if 200 people watching have just seen my ring piece, as well as probably my codpiece? Who cares?

With my back on the floor, I thrust him up even further into the sky. I've made my choice. I need to attack.

I want the weak me to die, to fritter away, to disintegrate. I came to this sport to learn how to become someone else, so that the old me would distance himself from the new me, like the multitudinous reflections you get when you look in a mirror with another mirror behind you. I came to Jiu-Jitsu to cut out all the traits of my personality that I was ashamed by.

The big man I'm now levering has gone crashing over sideways, rigidly, perplexed that he's been ripped out of his one-way path of pummelling the crap out of me.

Now, I have a choice. With him on his back, do I launch myself at him and try to crush him?

Or do I do something with his right leg that's now just in front of me, waiting to be grabbed?

I have milliseconds to work out what to do before he recomposes himself and comes back at me, re-attacking.

Do I act now, or do I continue to be reactive, to work out what the most technical thing to do in this moment could be?

No, I realise. I need to grab his ankle and put him in a leg lock. It's there for the taking.

The only problem is that since I got into trouble quite rightly at my gym all those months ago for trying to do knee bars thinking they were leg locks, I can't really remember how to attack the legs.

I haven't done a leg lock on someone for six months. Whereas before, where I could get someone to tap from a leg lock almost immediately, now I can't even remember the steps to pulling it off. I know you scoop your arm over and around their lower leg. But what do you do to finish the move?

Yet my opponent has composed himself now. His furious

body language means I need to refocus on his next attack. The problem is, I'm still trying to remember how to do a leg lock. And my brain can't handle thinking about two variables at once, under pressure and at speed.

So I grab his leg and I hope for the best. I'm just one move away from getting the gold medal and being able to legitimately call myself the English Champion. So maybe this will be the clincher for me, the moment I seal the gold.

I grip hold of his leg and shove it under my armpit then lean back. He frets and scrambles about, but he's got too much wiggle room. I'm doing something wrong clearly. I don't have any control over him. Normally the leg lock just comes straight on. I'm confused.

I shift my backside further up his leg so that my wrist is wrapped tighter around his ankle. Nothing still.

Oh, crikey. Come on! Tap!! Please!!

So I remember something vaguely about turning my body harshly to my left while still grabbing his leg. I do that. No, nothing. And now he's leaning forward towards me.

Quick! I turn my body almost all the way round so that surely he'll feel the leg-lock. In fact, I've turned around so much that I can barely see him.

And then he bounds up like an attacking lion and clambers all over my back, wraps his right arm around my neck and strangles me with both arms, squeezing as hard as he can. It's a rear-naked choke he's got on me. I've shown him too much of my back, and in doing so I'd loosened any pressure I'd had on his ankle and leg.

He squeezes my neck harder and harder until after about six seconds, the pressure is unbearable. I'm now sat back into him, my back pressed against his chest, and he's squeezing, squeezing, squeezing. I look up at the lights of the hall, and can see the blur of the crowd in front of me.

I don't want to tap. I don't want to tap. I don't want to. But there's no bloody way out.

I tap.

In disbelief and relief, the hairy monster dude who just

tapped me out whisper-screams to himself, "Yes!"

He's won the gold.

He leaps to his feet and holds his arm aloft.

Defeated, and no longer able to maintain 'Normal Face' now that the event is over for me, and I lost, I purse my lips together in a meek way. The referee holds our wrists, then raises his hand aloft.

The ref then looks at me, and to lift my spirits, makes a joke: "Well, at least all the spectators saw your arse."

I laugh, but the truth stings.

The bigger man won.

Humbled, I walk into his congratulatory embrace. We thank each other for the competition, and then walk back off the mat, shoulder to shoulder.

But to my shame, I find myself making a joke to him about what a big, heavy guy he is. "If we ever fight again, can you please make sure you don't weigh as much?"

He laughs and puts his arm around me, respectfully. To which I feel both grateful but also ashamed. I've been defeated so thoroughly, not just physically but also in spirit, that I can't stop prostrating myself before him. "Well done! You're the English Champion!"

His eyes flicker with acknowledgement but he's not getting carried away. We're only white belts.

But now I just can't bloody stop myself. Now stood on the podium, I say to him: "That's nice — that your wife and child got to see you win."

Wow. Crikey, Ben. Why don't you just go home and spend five hours baking him a cake? Or better still, why not just dress up like Marilyn Monroe and spring out of a cake to sing him happy birthday while stroking your big man tits? Honestly, enough. Stop. He beat you in a Jiu-Jitsu fight. He isn't a better person that you. He's just a guy who was better than you on the day, that's all. He capitalised on your mistakes. If you'd have had better technical ability, I told myself, you could have won.

Slowly, after proudly collecting my silver medal on the podium, I calm down, come back to myself and realise that when someone wins, they win in that moment; but they don't get ownership of how you perceive yourself or how you live your life.

I won silver. I was the bridesmaid, not the bride, today — but I could live with that.

On the podium, stood in second place, I bury the hatchet with the big man who, in an act of good grace, invites both myself and the 'Temporarily Scared Bloke with the Massive Back Who I Somehow Beat' in my first fight onto the podium's central, number one spot.

We hug, embrace and have a photo taken. 'Slightly Scared But Also Hard As Nails Bloke Who I Beat' comes over with his son, and we both express how relieved we are that that crap's all over with. He's a lovely guy, but for all the warmth, we do now all know our place within today's hierarchy. I could beat him in a fight today (but maybe not tomorrow) and the hairy monster who beat us both to gold continues to tower over us.

It's funny: when you've sweated and slobbered and crushed each other to bits and rubbed your trousered crotch all over each other's faces in pursuit of a medal, there's only really one way to go from there: up.

Together with your opponent you've shared an unmistakable and unforgettable slice in each other's lives and histories. People never forget that time they got into a fight, for better or for worse. The trauma becomes imprinted on their minds. And they certainly don't forget it when they're actually up against someone who has trained prior to that moment in order to get the better of them.

So win or lose, you and the guy you've fought share an unmistakable bond. Even if your actual fighting ability, in my case, may have been so shockingly non-technical that Jiu-Jitsu purists watching it might want to throw up.

Nevertheless, it meant something to me. And on my train journey home, while staring out of the window and eating an overrated Twix Duo, I reflect on how much Jiu-Jitsu has helped me release my personal demons into the ether.

Yes, I'm no longer as scared of getting beaten up as I used to be, but it's also taught me the importance of attacking, counter-attacking, and staying calm and strong of mind during an over-whelming attack upon my person..

Being submissive, and waiting to react to the next bad thing that happens to you isn't a good approach to BJJ, just like it isn't a good approach to life.

"Attack non-stop from now on," I tell myself. If you're attack-ing, you feel empowered. If you sit back and try to do the most technical thing possible, what you're really trying to do is en-gage your mind in a problem so that you don't have to think about attacking. In other words, if you're overthinking things, you're probably scared. Let your attack flow, I realise.

Instead, I re-emphasise to myself, just let it all flow from you — and attack! Which in common parlance means, 'Less think-ing, more doing,' itself a perfect metaphor for overcoming life's frustrations. For me, thinking is calming, but it also Segway's quite nearly into cowardice if one isn't careful. Often enemies have more respect for you, even when you lose, if you go down swinging. No one likes an easy win. So don't give it to them. I stare out of the train window and watch the fields whip by. I've been changed by this experience. I can feel it deep down.

CHAPTER SEVENTEEN

And yet — and yet! For all my personal insights and sense of perspective from getting beaten up at my second Jiu-Jitsu tournament, in the following days, my pride still hurt.

Yes, I was only a white belt; a stupid, know-nothing white belt. And sure, whether I won or lost at a tournament as a white belt meant absolutely nothing to anyone in the big scheme of things, or to anyone who actually knows anything about the sport.

But there's no denying that I'd trained my arse off for the past two years. I really hadn't cut any corners. I'd trained constantly. I'd sweated relentlessly. I really had given this sport my all. I'd tried to give it my 'Normal Face', and had tried to act like an expressionless Terminator robot on the mats, just like Jocko had said.

But when push had come to shove, I'd come up against a white belt with only two stripes on his white belt compared to my four stripes, and he'd battered me. And I couldn't understand how. I couldn't understand how I'd bottled it on such an epic scale, at the crucial moment. My 'Eye Of The Tiger' had closed up completely into a fearful squint.

It didn't matter that the guy who beat me had judo experience (desperate for answers, I looked him up on Facebook and saw a photo of him at a Judo academy).

Sure, he had muscles and he had all that height on me. But we were the same weight on the day, give or take. And height and muscles shouldn't come into it. We weighed the same, so I should have been able to deal with someone of equal weight. Plus Judo is mainly a stand-up sport, whereas Jiu-Jitsu is predominantly ground-based, so using his alleged Judo abilities as an excuse for my getting beaten up by him would have been beyond pathetic of me.

But the whole experience had shaken me up.

"This guy really roughed me up," I said to my wife in our kitchen, euphemistically scratching my head. "I don't understand what happened."

'You bottled it,' my mind replied. 'You shat your little Thomas the Tank Engine pants.' "Yeah, I just can't work it out..."

The following morning, despite having only had two fights in the previous day's tournament, together lasting no more than ten minutes, my entire body ached. It felt like I'd been panel-beaten by a hundred hammers.

Still, I couldn't shake it from my mind. I was one promotion away from becoming a blue belt. And I'd just got my arse handed to me by a white belt with only two stripes...

And so I decided to go straight back to the gym the next day and try to apply those lessons from the competition to my sparring sessions.

"Attack non-stop," I reminded myself. I'd failed to attack my opponent and it had cost me the gold.

So now, I decided I'd be all about attacking.

However, this newfound philosophy only got me so far on my first day back training. While sparring a new white belt with no stripes whatsoever, he kept repeatedly clambering onto my back and choking me out. I tried not to give my back to him at all, but it was just there for the taking, constantly.

What's more, while rolling with other white belts, if I didn't pay enough attention, I'd find myself in all kinds of precarious situations and wonder if I was now going to get tapped out by other white belts with virtually no experience whatsoever.

I was getting more of the fear that blue belts say they have where you begin to worry about losing face and self-respect in your own eyes for getting tapped by someone less experienced than you.

I also noticed that my new strategy of attacking non-stop like a wild man came with other flaws: it meant that I was now basically just flying across an opponent with no control, offering him all kinds of opportunities to sweep me off my feet, pin me to the mat and physically dominate me.

And heaven forbid I try this 'high-energy non-stop attack' nonsense on someone who's actually massive. Because when I did, against a very big, strong, high-level purple belt, he just laid on top of me with such heft alone that I immediately went into panic mode.

Unable to see anything underneath his mass, just on pressure alone, I tapped.

He was too big to use my strength against — though like a textbook white belt I tried to use all my strength in one big burst and was left in a sweaty heap on the mat.

In fact, when I'd applied my non-stop attack mode strategy to him, he'd just grabbed hold of me and squashed the life out of me, causing me to stick my arms out under him desperately, which he'd then bent back on themselves at uncomfortable angles until I'd tapped.

All of which really depressed me. I was now totally flummoxed about this BJJ game. "So," I surmised, "it appears that you have to be aggressive and keep applying the effort, and keep attacking, and always trying to take your opponent's back or take the mount (sit over him), but at the same time while using minimal energy so you don't wear yourself out?'

That seemed to be what the sport was suggesting, but I still found it all so mind-boggling that I did wonder at what point the fundamentals of Jiu-Jitsu might click together in my head.

Because, you see, my body was aching. My pride was hurt. My ego couldn't take it. And I just couldn't get my head around how to do Jiu-Jitsu but with such little energy that it feels like you're not doing it so you don't suddenly gas out and find yourself tapping out on claustrophobia, exhaustion and frustration combined.

Despite having done fairly well for a white belt at a national competition, it also felt like I'd regressed. Just when I thought I might actually know something, it turned out that actually I still knew nothing at all.

And so, adamant that I right the wrongs of my performance at the English Open, I signed up for yet another tournament: the ADCC British NOGI Open.

I felt the need to compete again.

I wanted to salvage my dignity.

CHAPTER EIGHTEEN

Three weeks later, I'm stood next to the Jiu-Jitsu mat, waiting to be called onto it by the ref. Alongside me is my next opponent. A younger guy in his early thirties, compared to me in my early forties, he limbers up. He looks a mixture of confidence and uncertainty, a weird kind of blend that nevertheless still manages to send a shiver of fear up my spine. What does he know? What can he do to me against my will? How scared should I be?

There are quite a few guys in my division at this event, but unlike before, I'm not letting my nerves completely get the better of me. I'm tell myself I'm going to fight the jitters, the mental fears and what-ifs. I'm going to be strong — by enjoying myself. By just being calm.

I'm going to go in there with an open heart.

I'm not sure why I've decided to suddenly start smiling and joking with people; why I've had a change of mind. But my subconscious seems to be saying to me: "You tried to be a tough guy in your last fight and it didn't work — you froze up. So maybe just try to be who you are."

And so that's what I do. I suddenly see the sport for what it is: a sport. It's not a vehicle for me to necessarily exercise all my childhood demons about getting bullied and beaten up, though it certainly has been both of those things.

In fact, Jiu-Jitsu is about expressing yourself in any way you want to, it seems. It's about being yourself as you execute the techniques that work for you.

Cut to moments later and I'm physically entwined with my opponent. The fight is on.

'So, right now, here on the mat, some big guy is trying to attack you,' I tell myself, as this human testament to the power of fast-twitch muscle fibre launches himself at me. Great! Hold him off and work around him. See what happens!'

And so that's what I do. As my opponent tries to grab hold of me to pull me to the ground, I grab him instead.

I put him in a guillotine, where I've got my arm wrapped around his neck and I'm choking him. The guillotine isn't on properly because I'm still rubbish at that technique even though it's really the only technique I have. But he's struggling.

After some exasperated panting on his part, though, his head pops out.

But unlike before, I don't panic. Like the Buddhists say, life is suffering, and life is about accepting that all kinds of bad things get thrown at you constantly. So the aim is to not fixate on them, but instead let your latest worry dissolve off you. To stay calm, instead of tensing up.

I do that. And although this guy is all over me, I'm thinking and I'm relaxed. I fly around to his back and put my full weight onto the side of his body as he rolls back onto his back.

He pushes me off him and then I push back with my weight but without unnecessary force. I'm doing my best to dominate him with technique and by flowing, instead of being reckless with my attack.

For the majority of the fight, though, it's just a mad scramble, him shocked he's not dominating a man ten years his senior, me pretty shocked about it too, given how physically strong this guy feels as we writhe, twist, grab, pull, kneel and strangle each other. If I saw him on the street, in the olden days I would have thought instantly that this guy could dominate me (and arguably even as an older man who now knows some Jiu-Jitsu).

But actually, when the fight is on, it often doesn't always play out like that. It's not about the size of the dog in the fight. It's not even about the size of the fight in the dog. It's about fighting non-stop for the past two-and-a-half years. The more you fight, the more used to it you become. You become inoculated to fighting. It doesn't matter your education, wealth, colour or creed. You can either fight a bit or you can't. And that comes from hours spent on the mat.

And for me, that realisation is an absolute thrill. The fact that the weakling at school can at any point completely change his view of the world and the world's view of them simply by learning how to fight like you might learn a subject at degree level, is fascinating. You can literally start again simply by learning BJJ, cutting out all the hurt from bullying in your past like it never really happened. It's an incredible realisation for me.

In the words of Jocko: "Oh, you want to fight? Fine. Fighting is my favourite thing to do." Although I'm still rubbish at it, I have to agree with Jocko. Of all the interests I have, fighting has become my favourite thing to do too.

On top of all these thoughts pinging around in my mind, I also can't believe I'm actually here, doing this, fighting this rough and tough-looking guy, and I'm just doing it! I'm not even screaming for my mummy, or whimpering, "Right, that's it! I'm calling the police!"

I'm fighting. This guy on top of me is trying to screw me up. He knows what he's doing, or he's certainly got some moves. But so what? He hasn't caught me yet. And it isn't over till it's over. Attack. Attack. Attack. Defend. Counter-attack. He tried to take my back and choke me. I'm move underneath him and he slides off me. Nearly! We both catch each others' eye, and smile at each other, as if to say to each other, "Oh yeah? Fuck you." God this sport is special.

That said, the thrill of being equally matched with my opponent in that moment gives way to a more truthful unfolding of events. Seconds later, he manoeuvres me around and he does take my back after all, just like the Big Hairy Dude did in my last fight at the English Open. He wraps his legs around my waist from behind, and tries to choke me with a reverse headlock — the rear-naked choke.

And he's really cranking my neck hard, getting his RNC on me deeper and deeper and deeper.

Trying to defend my neck, I've got my chin down so he doesn't wrap his full forearm around and into my throat. It's sort of working.

Gripping onto my back with his knees now, he realises he can't choke me like this as really he's got me in a headlock from behind, and now my nose is in the way. In fact, he's crushing my nose against my face and the only thing between him and victory is my bogey-maker.

So, placing his left hand flush against my forehead, he pulls my head skywards to pop my chin up in order to reveal more of my neck for him to choke.

But I won't give it to him. Screw it, I think. You'll have to crush my nose.

Out of the corner of my eye, I see the ref crouched down towards us looking closer to see if I'll tap.

But I'm now so loose emotionally in this fight, actually enjoying the rough and tumble of it, that I don't feel the need to tap.

Yes, he's really hurting my neck. I may even leave this tournament with a wonky nose. But I'm also at a distance from my emotions. And that feels great. Your feelings may not be facts, they say. And it's true. Because the fact is that I'm getting beaten up right now. But I feel great, about everything, like I'm soaring. I feel fantastic. I'm at one with myself.

Ironically, in this moment of both elation and physical struggle, I realise from out of the corner of my mind what my father was trying to tap into when he said to me as a boy: "Keep going forward throwing punches."

What he was really trying to say was that the toughest sportsmen have the courage to fight on.

That's what he meant! Not: keep charging at someone mindlessly who's going to beat the crap out of you, like that big kid did at my best friend's house when I was a child.

What my father said but I didn't fully grasp was: have the heart to stay in the fight. KEEP GOING! Yes, you may get hurt — in a fight with a bully, in a fight on the mats, in a fight with your own mind, in a battle with your own nerves.

But whatever you do: HAVE THE COURAGE TO FIGHT ON.

You don't need to grit your teeth, like I'd been doing metaphorically in life, and thrash around. Or try to be someone else like Jocko, a Navy Seal.

To be a man, to reach the peak of what it means to have character, you have to have the nerve to never surrender to your fears.

Because that's what your opponent is, I realise. He or she is just the manifestation of all your mental hang-ups.

You aren't fighting a person, per say. Ok, this guy is really squashing my nose right now. But actually, what I'm really fighting here is my inner voice that's always afraid.

Getting tapped out isn't a big deal if you know in your soul that you had the courage to keep going forward — that you didn't surrender to your own dark thoughts.

My dad's 'keep throwing punches' comment had been a metaphor.

It's not the dying that kills you — it's the terror of dying that rips you in half.

And sure, I never saw my father embrace this philosophy, because too often it's far easier said than done.

When that gigantic bloke who owned the laundrette would put my dad in a Full Nelson, with both my dad's arms tied behind my his back, sure, I didn't see my dad act like a hero and just tell the guy to stop.

But maybe his advice transcended that. Maybe it was the advice he wish he'd had the courage to act on himself, if only he'd been brave enough. Maybe also, the will to fight on was something he embraced in his own life like so many people do, just normal people, against all the odds, who still decide to get dressed the next day and head out of the door, even in the face of unbearable news.

Maybe that's what his advice meant: don't get knocked off course — push forward.

And so, trapped in this headlock, I do. I keep going. It's bad, the pain, but it's not that bad. I keep 'going forward' with it, even though I'm trying to figure a side-route out from it. Somewhere from here, I think, there must be a counterattack.

And so I try to wriggle my way out of it.

The ref shouts, "Time!" It's the end of the match.

I congratulate my opponent as I'm certain he won. He was the better fighter, certainly. I could just feel it. He was a bit stronger and was always a heartbeat ahead of me.

My opponent, though, blows out his cheeks: "That was hard work," he says to me, smiling but temporarily knackered. It's probably the biggest compliment he could have given me. My refusal to surrender has exhausted him; a definite silver lining for me, in spite of my loss.

Then the ref approaches me: "Mate, I don't know how you held off tapping to that choke he had on you. I would have tapped to that."

It's another huge compliment, and although I've lost the fight, I feel like a victor. I brought the fight to my opponent, and I showed heart.

I'm also extremely grateful to my vanquisher and to the ref for their feedback.

And although my opponent's hand is raised as the victor, I've completely made my peace with myself and the sport. Yes, I begrudged losing. But so what?

There was no shame in it. I'd given it my all. And ultimately I was grateful to this bloke. It was in his headlock that I realised what my dad had been saying to me all those years ago. The thing I was to fight was the 12-year-old illusory version of me in my mind that had held me back. I wasn't that boy anymore. I needed to let go of him. To move forward.

Yes, a part of me wanted to win that fight. I'd have liked to have won it in spectacular style. But I didn't.

And if I had won, would I have really won? Would I have learnt the lesson itself: that the enemy in life is often just your scared interpretation of events?

I'd lost a fight to learn that crucial life lesson. And when you put it like that, really, losing a Jiu-Jitsu match to learn an insight like that in many ways is a bargain. The insight is the victory.

What this tournament taught me was that the world isn't booby-trapped with people who are bigger than you, ready to fight you. Instead, the way forward, I realised, was to accept that sometimes things may get out of hand. But if you've inoculated yourself to the prospect of having to take care of yourself in a fight, then that's what Jiu-Jitsu gives you.

Buoyed by my epiphany, I focused my mind on my next bout.

I waited by the mats for my second fight — a battle for the bronze medal, for the honour of coming third.

Yet while standing there, I found myself next to the chap I was due to fight.

Instead of freezing up, though, I approached him and shook his hand. We had a very amicable chat, him telling me that in his previous fight he would have won if the last guy he'd fought hadn't kept illegally poking him in the eyes.

But as we talked it dawned on me that I was now doing exactly the opposite of what I did at the English Open. I wasn't doing Normal Face. I wasn't tense. I was just completely loose and being myself; floating along the top of the ocean with the mindset, "Well, what will be will be."

Instead of feeling a sense of betrayal for letting my mind take me hostage as it usually does before altercations, I just felt all loosey-goosey. I was at peace.

Fast forward five minutes, and my next fight starts. And I go for it, not in my usual white-knuckle-howling-banshee style, but instead in a more meditative way. I try to fight aggressively but to not overthink it. I try to be ruthless but at one with the process. I try to let things flow (as best they can when you have virtually no techniques in your head).

And for a while, as with my previous opponent, we're evenly matched. I stand up and he sweeps me down onto the mat. I control his body but then he catches me within his legs.

But what's so remarkable about this whole experience, this battle for third place, is that I no longer care that there's a crowd. I'm just having fun and doing my thing. I'm just like Keanu Reeves in The Matrix, but bald, old and with tits.

And although the prospect of now coming fourth in the category looms large, and I'm forced to consider the prospect of going home with my tail between my legs, the truth is that I'm not afraid of being in the dragon's lair anymore. I'm not afraid of fighting.

I can feel it within me.

I know I'm crap at Jiu-Jitsu. I know I'm not a great fighter. But I'm fine with that. I don't feel I have to defend myself or my honour or the nervous 12-year-old boy within me. That huge figure of self-doubt and fear of physical contact doesn't scare me anymore. As sad as I am that I didn't stand up for myself as a child when I was younger, I don't feel that same burning sense of shame anymore. In fact, my bullies lead me to this point. In many ways, I owe them.

The guys here today like in all Jiu-Jitsu tournaments have come to give it their all in heart and mind, and my current opponent is no different. These fighters have trained their arses off so that they're in peak physical condition, their minds also as strategically sharp in the fight as possible.

And yet, me; the now 41-year-old me; old, greying bearded me whose wedding ring won't fit on his left hand properly anymore because I've got sausage fingers from eating too much M&S Dine In For Two... I'm absolutely fine. In fact, I feel spectacular.

I may have been used for personal gain by muggers when I was a kid. My best friend as a child may have betrayed me in my childish mind by letting his friends bully me, and not said anything while I got beaten up in front of him. But like me, I realise, he was scared too.

The people I may have deeply trusted as friends as a little boy may have hurt me because I put too much trust into them. But now that's fine, I realise.

I will maintain my ethics and my principles and not stoop low and blame others. I'll stop dwelling on it.

After 29 years, I'm ready to move on. And if, one fateful day, push comes to shove once the talking stops and I'm forced into an altercation and there's no way out, then for once and at last in life, I'm fine with that too. I realise that my favourite thing to do in life now also is fighting.

My opponent and I continue to roll around, and although he's more technical than me, I can see his moves before he does them, allowing me to defend them as I press forward with my attack.

He tries to take my back but I turn into him and block his hips.

Now in his triangle, with his legs wrapped around my neck, I manage to escape. I roll off him and then grab his right foot.

I go for the leglock. But as I'm grabbing his foot, I leave my legs exposed too and so now he grabs my right leg.

As we both attempt to turn away in the opposite direction so that the foot lock comes on quicker on our opponent, my newfound nemesis does what I forget to do: clamp my knees together around his one knee and thrust our hips upwards.

But at my end, holy cow, the sudden pain in my leg is excruciating. So I tap.

My opponent doesn't feel my tap, though, and the ref doesn't see it. So, in a high-pitched voice, with my back arched as I'm in so much agony, I shout-squeal, "Tap!"

My opponent lets off the pressure, the ref urgently separates us, and we both stand.

I congratulate my opponent, both of us very relaxed in body language, and his left hand is held up as the victor.

But, as we both walk off the mats, both having shared the farty, breathy, sweaty, cheesy-feetness of each other's struggling humanity, the funny thing is that I don't feel like the loser, or even 'a loser.'

Again, I feel like I won.

Jiu-Jitsu has revealed in me all the things I feared most about myself. It's allowed me to confront my past.

As a boy, I was like a blank canvas who took the world at face value. And when I was bullied, it rearranged me in a certain screwed up way. It reordered the foundations of my personality in a way that meant my character — my personality — was built skew-whiff.

And every time I found myself in an altercation, my sense of hurt at being fed to the lions every time I visited the home of my best friend was ripped open again.

Every time as an adult someone had a disagreement with me, or worse — like that bloke at the train station or the skinheads in the car — and they just wanted to bash my head in, the former me, the person stood there, looking up at my assailant, was the confused 12-year-old version of me hidden in my grown man's body.

But actually, I realise, the only person who betrayed me was me, and my former approach to the world.

Am I to still blame the 17-year-old who picked me up by my nipples and the tip of my penis after I attacked him for throwing matchboxes and cigarette papers at my head?

No. He was just a boy, too.

And actually, I realised, as I washed and dressed myself in the event's locker rooms, my friend who was too scared to jump in and help me from his other friends helped conceive the person I am now.

And yet, although I'd just lost yet another fight, few things are supposedly more nerve-wracking than fighting someone else — especially someone who knows that he's doing.

And I'd overcome that fear almost completely. Instead, I was now relaxed, and I enjoyed it for the fun — for the truth-seeker — that it is.

After more than a quarter of a century plagued by fear, I felt cleansed.

CHAPTER NINETEEN

Four weeks later I'm driving through the area where my parents live, my mind lost in thought. I'm listening to music, absently dwelling on my obligations for the day ahead.

And then I see him. It's my old best mate from when I was a child, the one who was understandably too scared to defend me as a child when I was bullied and getting picked up by my bellend by that older boy in his bedroom.

He's tall now, skinny, and his face is screwed up in a tight mess. Something is troubling him, playing on his mind.

He was my sidekick, and I was his. We were both Robin, with no Batman in sight.

But now, all I see is a frustrated middle-aged man, dressed in painter-and-decorator overalls, a 42-year-old man heading into his fifth decade, life playing with his thoughts.

I realise that since we last saw each other when we were children, there has been so much water under the bridge. So many more — and far more instructive — events have happened in both of our lives, forming who we've become as adults.

As hurt as I was by his failure to intervene or even say something when his friends were bullying me, to now confront him as an adult and ask for an apology for something he failed to do when he was a child seems ridiculous.

It is ridiculous. He did nothing wrong. Would I have stepped in if I were him? Of course not. So who am I to try and hold the boyhood version of him to a higher standard than I'd ever dream of holding myself?

We were children. We're now at an age where our loved ones are either entering the final stages of their lives and are being broken down by gravity and slowly packed off out of this world like used Amazon delivery boxes the evening before bin day.

Life is tragic, even if it's interspersed with breathtaking moments of unassailable magic, whether it's cuddling your children or sweating out life's grime in a sparring session on the mats.

We all carry boulders from our past. Just because he was in the room when someone loaded one of those boulders of injustice onto my back doesn't mean he was the boulder itself. I chose to feel like a victim. That had been my mistake.

The fact that he didn't step forward to stop them just meant he was human. He wasn't my crucifix. And he didn't give me this cross to bear.

My interpretation of the harshness of life had been my real enemy, and life didn't give a damn then and it doesn't give a damn now. You're in control of how you view the world.

And yet, without that piercing moment of pain in my best friend's bedroom — both the pain in my left nipple and the tip of my bell-end, as well as the pain I felt at my friend's alleged betrayal, there would have been no Jiu-Jitsu in my life. No solution.

Life may have delivered that pain to me, and made my former best friend the symbol of that sudden rush of awareness of life's cruel ways as a child. But I let it linger.

However, that same ebb and flow of the universe also offered me a solution to my 30-year-long sense of injustice by throwing me a white belt and saying, "Here, you fat, whiny turd: try BJJ..."

Plus, cut back to me in the car, on a practical level, if I now honk my horn at my old best friend walking towards me on the pavement as I'm driving past, and instead pull my car over for a chat, what will I say?

What is there to say?

We're both entirely different people, even if we resemble the embers of our past.

If it's said that all the cells in our bodies die and are replaced with new ones every seven years, then what does that say about our personalities?

We're entirely different beings now. I'm not the same person I was two years ago, when I started Jiu-Jitsu, never mind three decades ago.

And so, if I were to pull over and make small talk with him, who would I be making small talk as: the 12-year-old who got beaten up in his bedroom, or the 41-year-old who can sort of — almost — defend himself in a fight?

My stomach turns with the realisation that the 12-year-old boyhood version of me from my past is dying. That boy barely exists anymore. That childhood version of me is vanishing.

A sense of deep sadness and mourning comes over me, like an acknowledgement of the relentless passing of time.

So I hesitate at the wheel. Should I try to reconnect with my old friend, to seek out some kind of closure that I may or may not get from us speaking again after what feels like a lifetime?

I feel myself drawn to the prospect of reconnecting again, magnetised to my past.

Although I'm an adult encaging my boyhood self, the departing spirit of my youth finds itself in all its innocence and lack of defence trying to force itself from my body.

I find myself yearning for acceptance, to get closure for the blank sheet of A4 that was my childhood self, before my metaphorical piece of white paper, my young soul, had become ink-stained, dog-eared and tatty.

I hear the voice in my mind begging me to pull my car over, to make connections, to slot together emotionally like Duplo blocks, to bond over our shared past.

The hurt child in me wants to start again. With a heaviness in the depths of my stomach, the temptation is overpowering.

But I stop myself. The hourglass keeps emptying, it dawns on me.

Yet I've been trapped in another time. I realise that it's tomorrow that you need to focus on, not dwell on a past or a personality that barely exists.

I'd been living my whole life with my mind stuck on pause, on that one scene. An incident that had lasted no more than three minutes was still having ramifications — and big ones for me — nearly 16 million minutes later.

After nearly half a century of life, it was time for me to grow up and become a man. Those wounds had virtually healed, and Jiu-Jitsu had been both the plaster and then my nurse.

It was time for me to stop being enslaved by my past.

I had been reborn increment by increment with each new stripe on my white belt. I had chipped away at that rock of injustice on my back with every single class of Jiu-Jitsu I'd attended.

The boy in my soul that I always feel an invisible tie to will always be there, bursting through my adult personality in shards, because that is the foundation of who I was.

But the un-seeable marionette strings that bound me to that hurt 12-year-old who'd controlled me in adulthood had now been cut, I realised. I was free from that hurt.

If the art of Jiu-Jitsu is about working around the problem rather than getting destroyed my facing it head on, then ironically Jiu-Jitsu is the thing in itself that helped me circumnavigate my pain. I wasn't scared of fighting: I was trapped in a scene from my past where fighting was involved.

By learning Jiu-Jitsu, I realise with excitement, I'd found a way to fight life at its own game.

I had saved my soul. Without BJJ, I wouldn't be sat in this car right now, wearing an English Open Jiu-Jitsu competition t-shirt underneath my casual shirt to keep me warm.

I wouldn't have that little recess in my brain constantly working in overtime, thinking about Jiu-Jitsu techniques while my mind is engaged elsewhere in everyday issues.

What doesn't kill you makes you stronger, I remind myself, as I grip my steering wheel with forearms strengthened by Jiu-Jitsu.

Life isn't about just accepting your place as a cog in the machine. It's about finding freedom within yourself on your own terms; to find an outlet to be, do, think and express yourself in a way that feels true to you; that helps you gather up all those bad past experiences like kindle and use them to light a fire in your soul.

Yes, I was still a white belt after two years. I was still a beginner in the big scheme of things. But I was at peace with who I'd become. I'd made my peace with my past. I could see through the puzzle of my own self-deception. I'd done myself proud.

Even if I were to stay at white belt forever, I realised, it wouldn't matter. The real prize was inner change.

I relax my body and decide to drive straight past my old friend, heading out from under the clearing of these trees overhead.

I'm on a new path now, buoyed by the prospect of seeing all the fond sights and sounds of my Jiu-Jitsu club at class this evening, where all the toxins of my history have been washed off.

I'll slap and bump fists with training partners, roll hard and get choked and tapped. And then we'll all hug and laugh about it afterwards like it was no big thing, even though my training partner and I have just glimpsed into each other's souls — and he'll have inevitably won.

We'll laugh at the mistakes we made on the mats because we'll know it's making us better, stronger people.

That's the beauty of Jiu-Jitsu. That's how it works.

The boys who had bullied me had been as malleable as me. They weren't villains, they too were life's victims — they were human. All too human.

As kids, they'd been reacting to life's traumas, just like in adulthood I'd been reacting to theirs.

To experience pain — and yet to survive it — is to understand what it means to be human.

"Let go, or be dragged," goes the saying. Let go, and let time runs its course. Everything fades.

I glimpse in my rear view mirror at the back of my old friend now behind me, then stare at the wide open road ahead.

And I do what every Jiu-Jitsu practitioner does when he sees a path towards someone's back.

I put my foot down on the pedal, hard — and I attack.

Printed in Great Britain
by Amazon

56515590R00099